Write On!

First published in 2007 by New Holland Publishers (UK) Ltd
London • Cape Town • Sydney • Auckland

www.newhollandpublishers.com

Garfield House, 86-88 Edgware Road, London W2 2EA, United Kingdom
•
80 McKenzie Street, Cape Town 8001, South Africa
•
14 Aquatic Drive, Frenchs Forest, NSW 2086, Australia
•
218 Lake Road, Northcote, Auckland, New Zealand

2 4 6 8 10 9 7 5 3 1

ISBN 978 1 84537 706 9

Editorial Director: Jo Hemmings
Editors: Gareth Jones and Kate Parker
Assistant Editor: Giselle Osborne
Designer: Rod Teasdale/White Rabbit Editions
Production: Hema Gohil

Cover reproduction by Pica Digital PTE Ltd, Singapore
Printed and bound in India by Replika Press Pvt. Ltd

Write On!

Martin Gurdon

Contents

1 **The Truth About Writing**   6
Why it's not as hard as you think

2 **That's Enough About You, Let's Talk About Me**   12
How I became a writer

3 **The Basics, Part 1**   18
News writing – who, what, why, when and where?

4 **The Basics, Part 2**   39
Feature writing – essays for grown-ups

5 **Cut the Crap**   59
How to self-edit

6 **The Curse of the Cliché**   70
How to escape from hackneyed hell

7 **An Explanation of Punctuation**   78
Every dot and comma

8 **Grammar School**   97
Taking the grind from grammar

9 **Pitch Perfect**   105
How to sell story ideas

10 **Life as a Freelance Writer** 117
Self-help for self-starters

11 **Freelance Journalism** 125
A working life

12 **Legal Aid** 129
Writing and the law

13 **A View From the Sub's Bench** 136
The experts' experts reveal all

14 **Work Station** 144
How to drag order from chaos

15 **The Key** 150
Forget your fears and enjoy your words

Further Reading 152

Useful Websites 154

Index 155

Acknowledgements 160

Chapter 1

THE TRUTH ABOUT WRITING
Why it's not as hard as you think

Does the idea of writing fill you with dread? Do you feel a sense of thwarted ambition when it comes to putting words on a page? You needn't. Most of us write, even if what we write is a shopping list, a postcard or a diary entry. We may not think about the processes used to create these things, but generally they're available to us. Beyond basic, functional writing, we might have ambitions to produce words for a report, a newsletter or even a piece of journalism. Getting them correctly onto the page is not just the province of professional writers, and none of us is excluded from the skills required to do this well.

However, if you don't have these skills, the methods involved in ordering information, and finding the words to get it across can seem mysterious, frustrating and daunting. You may recognise good writing, but feel that you don't understand the elements that create it. Punctuation might cause you problems, or you may lack the ability to unscramble data so that what goes on the page tells the reader what you want it to.

Any discomfort you feel about writing could simply be because you haven't written anything for years, and find the process awkward and embarrassing when it's forced on you now. People have strong opinions on what they consider to be good writing, and will berate those they believe fall short. It's very tempting to avoid putting yourself in the firing line of such comments.

I once worked for a newspaper, the editor of which was regularly assailed by letters from a man who liked nothing better than to obsessively dissect articles and stories, hoping to track down any mistakes in structure and punctuation, which he would then gleefully report with righteous fury – copying what he had written to a story's author, the better to ruin his or her day. The subtext of his letters was always the same: 'You have been useless and incompetent, and I have found you out.'

Ruth Rendell, the crime novelist, produced a story about a similar character, who wrote to authors about their mistakes, listing the tiniest errors. She described his other more unattractive social tendencies with such force that you might have suspected the narrative had a personal subtext.

Our newspaper's literary pedant was often spot on, but on many occasions his observations were eccentric or simply wrong, and those who received them – including me – had to resist the temptation to correct his letters and send them back. Sometimes such people have a point, even if they are at the nuttier end of the human spectrum. Rotten, lazy writing is infuriating, and frequently comic, as we'll discover, but there can often be an element of power play tied up in this sort of criticism, and as most of us have discovered, it's hard to learn from something when it's delivered with a sneer.

> 'With a little practice a lot of people would easily be capable of producing decent, workman-like writing, but fear being exposed as "not knowing".'

With a little practice a lot of people would easily be capable of producing decent, workman like writing, but fear being exposed as 'not knowing', so avoid learning, sometimes developing ingenious strategies to conceal knowledge gaps. The irony is that if the same ingenuity was applied to plugging those skills gaps then they could probably be sorted out pretty quickly.

There is no shame in not knowing something: in this case how to write. All this means is that you have yet to find out. 'Not knowing' simply provides you with the opportunity of doing the necessary research, but if you start the learning process from the position of thinking, 'I should know X at my age' or 'I didn't know Y, and it's so obvious that I must be stupid', then you are creating barriers to learning and setting yourself up to fail.

Yes, there are recognised parameters that define the writing process, but there are no 'shoulds' and 'musts' about how many of them you know already, or how easy they are to learn now. So relax, bin any preconceptions, and you will make progress. How much progress? Sometimes this is difficult to measure, but allowing yourself the luxury of thinking, 'I still don't quite get this' at any point as you read this book, then stopping and analysing why, will give you the space to learn.

> **'Treat your mistakes as friends to be embraced, studied and learned from rather than denied and avoided.'**

You will make mistakes. This is good, because they show you how to develop and improve. Once you understand why something does not work, then you can avoid it in the future or correct it. The novelist Ernest Hemingway is said to have spent days honing two or three paragraphs, cutting out words that he felt were useless, rearranging ideas, working at getting the commas, full stops and other punctuation paraphernalia just so. He wrote in longhand – standing up, oddly enough – and his manuscripts have a mass of scribbled corrections and amendments. This implies that he saw room for improvement and development in his writing, that he found mistakes in what was originally written. This does not make Hemingway a bad writer.

If you start with the perspective that everything you write should be instantly perfect, and that error equals weakness, then you are creating a very personal strait-jacket which will restrict your ability to get things right. Treat your mistakes as friends to be embraced, studied and learned from rather than denied and avoided, and they will help you. With practice you will make them less frequently, and they will increasingly become absent friends.

There is no escape from practice I'm afraid. Just as musicians, dancers and actors need to rehearse to keep their talents and techniques sharp, so writers must churn out words to gain and maintain the experience needed to use them properly. Practical experience is always the best teacher.

'Remember that at some point in their lives even the world's greatest journalists and writers knew less about their craft than you do now.'

If at times you find the information contained in this book hard going, struggle to understand some of the concepts it contains, or decide some of its contents may not work for you, none of this will matter if you free yourself from worrying about it, and take pleasure in what you *have* learned. Remember that at some point in their lives even the world's greatest journalists and writers knew less about their craft than you do now.

You may genuinely want to write – ache to write in fact – rather than have to do so, but find the elegant sentences that tumble round inside your head turn leaden and messy when translated onto the page. *Write On!* will provide the information you need to get beyond this depressing process.

I've written the book from a journalist's rather than an author's perspective, although you will find some overlap between the two disciplines. There are specific rules and practices involved with journalism that can usefully be employed in almost any form of writing. These techniques remove flab from sentences and add clarity to the information they contain. Many of these 'trade secrets' are easily accessible. Making use of them generally requires no great knowledge, and once grasped, they are liberating.

You will also find quite a lot of references to freelance journalism, because this is a form of professional writing that requires large dollops of self motivation, organisation and creativity to make it work. Many struggling authors would struggle less if they approached their craft with the pragmatism of good freelance journalists. Using a mix of personal experience and interviews, *Write On!* shows how this can be done.

Hacking it

There are some brilliant journalists who are not great writers. Their skills are channelled into getting to the nub of a subject and making it interesting and explicable. They do this by a mixture of research, self-editing and grasping the facts that are at the core of a story.

We've all read fuzzy, circular things that never get to the point, because they're drowning in a sea of cluttered thought. Occasionally they can be beautifully written (although often they are not: flannel, padding and lousy writing frequently go together), but if something has no substance, or that substance is chopped up and spread over several paragraphs so that it's lost, then reading it is a waste of time. Frankly, so is writing it.

Using a mix of personal experience, received wisdom and skills learned from 20-something years of getting into print in magazines and newspapers, I hope to help you avoid falling into these and many other literary black holes.

If writing professionally, or semi-professionally, appeals to you – perhaps combining a skill or interest with freelance journalism – there are chapters that explain the most effective ways to do so. If not, these chapters will still help you to apply a professional sheen to anything you do write. So whatever your interests, don't skip them and move on.

Change your life. Perhaps.

This book does not promise to make you the next Ernest Hemingway or editor of *Vogue*, or to transform the act of producing the written word from drudgery into artistic endeavour, nor does it claim that you can become rich and fulfilled from writing – although all these things are possible. What it will do is make the process easier, and potentially more enjoyable as a result.

Some of what this book contains is subjective and opinionated, and you might not agree with every single word, but thinking about why you disagree can help you to re-evaluate the way you write, and why you think certain things work on the page and others don't. This can help make you a better writer on your own terms.

- **Writing is not a black art. You don't need an English degree to enjoy it.**

- **There's no shame in not knowing how to do something others find easy. We all have different skills.**

- **Don't fear failure. Learning from mistakes is useful and productive.**

- **Practice is essential. Simply reading this book won't make you a better writer.**

- **Enjoy the process when it's fun; keep going when it's not.**

Chapter 2

THAT'S ENOUGH ABOUT YOU, LET'S TALK ABOUT ME
How I became a writer

I am a freelance journalist, a hack writer. Most of my professional existence involves filling up the white space between the advertisements in newspapers and magazines. I am not a 'name' writer. Nobody reads my stuff because I've written it. They read it because it tells them something useful, interesting or entertaining. Mostly, I am a conduit for information, and earn a living by the way I get that information across.

The words I write need to be well crafted, and lock together like the pieces of a jigsaw puzzle to create a cohesive whole. They should also be accurate. If they're not, then I'm in trouble. Generally, the person who has commissioned a freelancer only notices him or her if the piece he or she has written is incorrect. You're only as good as the last thing you've written.

Freelance journalists operate in a competitive, crowded market. A lot of people would like to be part of that market, which makes most of us infinitely disposable and replaceable, and our working lives permanently insecure. To survive, I need a degree of clear-eyed detachment from what I'm writing, which allows me to change any element of it to give those who have commissioned me what they want. It needs to be the right length, and contain the facts I said it would, or the things they asked for. If it does not, there are plenty of people willing to fill the brief and take my place.

Working as a freelance journalist is rather like being a shark. You're constantly on the move: chasing work, generating work, following up possible work. If you stop, you die.

I've had stints as a reporter for obscure trade magazines, been a freelance feature writer and a commissioning editor for a newspaper supplement, and to varying degrees have made a success of these, but have no illusions that the work is ever going to make me vast sums of money. There are freelancers who are very comfortably off, thanks to particular skills, specialist knowledge, good contacts, high profiles, or simply a superhuman ability to come up with ideas, chase work and produce thousands of words, week after week, year after year, without lowering their standards or burning out. Some are simply very talented.

Bad example

The route I took into journalism is not one I'd recommend to anyone else. Since the age of 13 I'd wanted to be a motoring writer, as words and cars were my two particular interests, and a magazine called *Car* elegantly mixed both.

The combination of writing about a subject that interested me and getting paid for it seemed an impossible dream, but it was rather an inspirational one as well. Schooling wasn't, and when my formal education finished I was 16 and had one meagre qualification – a now defunct British exam called a CSE, generally taken by the less academic, and seen by many employers at the time as next to useless. Mine was a Grade 2 in History, and never did me much good.

Most of my friends headed off to university, but a career in journalism did not beckon, and I spent several years in menial jobs. These included working as a bicycle delivery boy for an optician, selling dustbin bags over the telephone and working as a messenger boy for the Press Association news agency, delivering photographs to the editorial offices of national British newspapers in the days before this was done electronically.

The papers were still grouped in and around London's Fleet Street, often in grand buildings with basements that still rumbled to the sound of ancient printing presses, and the noise of compositors making up old style 'hot metal' pages, which were basically like giant, metallic ink stamps filled with the newspaper pages. In the early 1980s there wasn't a word processor to be seen – although they existed – and editorial offices still echoed with the clatter of hefty, manual typewriters, usually being pounded by chain-smoking men who used two fingers to type.

My colleagues and I passed virtually unnoticed through the editorial offices. We supplied a resource, and our existence barely registered with the people who worked in these places, which meant I was surrounded by journalism, but utterly detached from it and intensely frustrated as a result.

Doorstepping

I was 19 and going nowhere when I approached *Car* magazine with some story ideas. I visited their offices, which were within walking distance of where I worked. The editor was away and I was asked to send him a letter – email had yet to arrive.

'Somebody from a motoring magazine has phoned you,' said my grandmother when I got home from work a few days later.

Returning the call I was almost shaking with excitement. The man I spoke to was the editor. He said I'd shown initiative by visiting his office and had written an articulate letter. He asked my age, then told me he was 33 'and rather old'. I thought this was true, but did not say so. Although he wasn't interested in the ideas I'd offered, he asked if I'd produce 1,000 words on a 1930s' Fiat and give them to him in a week.

I couldn't type, so dug out old magazines, phoned Fiat and an owners' club for the cars and scrawled out a story in longhand. Job done, I thought.

Wrong. My father, bless him, made me read this *magnum opus* aloud. I tripped up over stray commas and badly placed full stops. The way information seesawed illogically through the story and the clunking attempts at humour were also cruelly exposed.

I'd learned one of the novice writer's most valuable lessons. What you think you've written isn't necessarily what's on the page. Reading aloud meant that I really had to listen to the words I'd produced. Silent reading often means 'skim' reading. Your brain thinks it knows what it's seeing, so sails blithely over the details, whether they're good or bad.

> **'I'd learned one of the novice writer's most valuable lessons. What you think you've written isn't necessarily what's on the page.'**

My teenage ego took a battering, but having given up arguing that my first attempt at professional writing worked, I rewrote it again and again, on the train to work and in the periods between trudging around Fleet Street. Each evening, once my dog-tired father got back from his job, we'd work into the small hours, as he made me read and reread, listening to the rhythm of the sentences I'd churned out, justifying every comma and full stop. My dad knew I was in a hole, and realised that this story had the potential to allow me to at least begin climbing out of it.

Try and try again

How many rewrites did this involve? I can't remember now, but it was something like 10 or 15 before I finally gave the end product to a typist friend who squinted at my messily looping handwriting and transcribed it onto sheets of A4 paper.

Three months later and I was in print for the first time and feeling a mixture of intense relief and utter delight, as this inconsequential little story about a car I hadn't actually seen seemed to indicate that I could earn a living from something I loved doing.

A mixture of complete naïveté about the workings of the publishing industry and magazine production, social skills to die for (being immature and verbally clodhopping, I frequently did die socially), and crass expectations that work would start flooding in, meant I spent another five years in part-time jobs. I hobbled along on infrequent freelance writing commissions, and then put in a stint as an inept public relations copywriter, before finally landing a proper writing job as a reporter on a fortnightly trade magazine for personnel officers, where I belatedly received the journalistic training most of my colleagues had enjoyed years before.

By that stage I was poor, frustrated and very lucky to have been given this career lifeline. I wasn't writing about cars, but I was now writing a great deal, and learning a lot in the process. For the first time, I had to work to regular deadlines, make my words fit the magazine's house style and write a mix of news, feature stories and profiles. My colleagues were ambitious, talented and supportive – my immediate boss soon left to join the BBC's *Newsnight* programme. None of them were interested in the grovelling expediency often associated with trade magazines, tied as they are to a limited readership and limited income from a small group of advertisers. The first six months at the magazine were an adrenalin rush of learning, and like the *Car* magazine story, much of what I learned at that time is still relevant to the work I do now.

Freedom

Four years and two jobs later, I went freelance, endured another very lean period, then gradually began picking up work from *The Big Issue*, a news and features magazine sold by homeless people, and the *Guardian* newspaper, where I made my national daily newspaper debut. I was writing about cars again – an odd thing to do for *The Big Issue*, but there you go – now applying the researching and writing skills I had picked up in the trade press. Then, when *The Daily Telegraph* launched a weekly motoring supplement with a voracious appetite for freelancers capable of supplying story ideas, I was delighted to help them fill the gaps. In the process, this got my work under the noses of people who hadn't seen it before, and I was able to expand my contacts book and outlets still further.

'If you have to look at the good and bad points of someone else's words, this inevitably feeds back into your own work.'

I've been self-employed ever since, even while spending a couple of years helping to edit a motoring supplement for the *London Evening Standard*, which involved editing colleagues' words for the first time. Eighteen years after first getting into print, this was one of the most instructive, thought-provoking processes I'd experienced as a writer. If you have to look at the good and bad points of someone else's words, this inevitably feeds back into your own work.

Today, I'm back writing from home, producing a mixture of journalism and books. I still try to start each day on the basis that you're only as good as the last thing you wrote, that there's always interest to be wrung from the driest subject – it's a sanity clause when confronted with being asked to produce 2,000 words on say, giving employees cash instead of company cars – and that putting words to work is one of the most satisfying ways to spend your time. Although I don't always feel it, I'm extremely lucky to get paid for the privilege.

- **There are many good writers who've come to the subject from other disciplines.**

- **Lacking a track record and relevant qualifications, however, won't have helped them.**

- **If you're keen to write for a living, then taking any necessary exams is probably the easiest route.**

Chapter 3

THE BASICS, PART 1
News writing – who, what, why, when and where?

There are two main forms of journalistic writing, news and
feature writing, with the first often informing the latter.
Understanding the differences between them, and the rules
of each, will help with any writing you have to produce.
So even if your aspirations are towards literary work, don't
skip this chapter, because a lot of the advice it gives
will be useful to you.

Let's start with news stories of the sort that you see in the front of
newspapers. They tell you about events succinctly and in a very
specific way, even if the styles and slants vary. The word 'news' is itself
a derivative of 'new', so a news story is always about a new happening,
event or comment. Even if that event has already taken place it can
generate more news stories as its effects and consequences make
themselves felt and the story develops.

Never-ending story

'Man shot in restaurant' is a news story. 'Man taken to hospital' – that's
another. 'Doctors fight to save man's life' and 'Desperate search to find
rare blood type for shot man' – two more. 'Man dies' – bad luck for
the man, but he's already the subject of story number five. Six comes
with the arrest of his wife, and her subsequent release will cause even
more column inches to be written, and you can bet her furious

comments will then generate further news stories.

Fast forward 12 months. The man's killers still haven't been found and his unsolved death causes a senior policeman to call for a change in the gun laws, resulting in more headlines about firearms. A defensive quote from a politician charged with overseeing those gun laws carries the debate forward into the legal arena – because her views impact on laws that affect all of us, what she says is newsworthy even if she thinks the laws are fine as they are – and so yet another story results from the comments she makes.

> **'Follow the simple mnemonic "who/what/why/when/where?" when approaching the content of a news story, and you won't go far wrong.'**

Meanwhile, the restaurant where the man ate his last supper has seen a 20-per-cent increase in trade since his murder, with customers booking the table where he sat. This unsavoury behaviour amongst the sweetmeats will fill acres of news print. This has become a story about ghoulish behaviour, and the latest quotes and opinions expressed about this worrying trend will keep it alive for weeks. By now the newest element of this self-perpetuating series of events has nothing much to do with the poor sod who was bumped off in the first place.

Tools for the job

Follow the simple mnemonic 'who/what/why/when/where?' when approaching the content of a news story, and you won't go far wrong. This is a great way to distil or simplify written information, making it clear in your mind what it is you're writing about. To start with this won't necessarily be obvious, sometimes because there's a lack of hard fact, sometimes because there's so much of it that choosing what to put in or leave out is difficult. Making a brief list before you start, using the 'who/what/etc.' headings will often clarify things.

Then decide on the story's most important element, its 'news point'. This should be the subject of the opening paragraph. It could be any of these things: prominent person says something important (who); lost dog found (what); rule change prevents parents parking outside school (why); statue unveiled today (when) in the high street (where). There's room for some personal interpretation here – the story about the statue could come under the heading of 'what' or 'why' – but there's a certain satisfaction in deciding how to order the information at your disposal. It will also prevent you from missing out important facts, waffling or repeating stuff – all common errors found in stories where the writer isn't confident that he or she is on top of the subject, or hasn't properly thought through what he or she is trying to say.

When I was being trained to write news, two things were impressed on me with, more or less, verbal jackboots. One was that the word 'new' should never be used in a news story – 'if it isn't new why are you writing about it?' was the refrain. Newness was a given. Secondly, the opening paragraph should tell you exactly what the rest of the story is about (in other words its news point), and all the following paragraphs should explain and amplify that news point. That first paragraph should also be short and concise. Twenty-five words was considered ideal, and 35 the absolute maximum.

> 'The opening paragraph should tell you exactly what the rest of the story is about.'

Not all newspapers follow the rule about length, which tends to apply more to tabloids. Some 'serious' papers have been known to have opening news story paragraphs of a hundred words, but keeping things short is actually a very good discipline. If you can summarise the most important element of your story in 25 words then there's a good chance you've really got a handle on what it's about.

In some countries, the word 'tabloid' is almost a term of abuse, being associated with sensationalist and intrusive writing, but it also refers to a specific way of putting together information on the page as simply as possible. Doing this well is, in its way, as much of a skill as great poetic writing. The fact that it looks simple does not make it simple in practice.

What's the story?

You may have to write about something that lacks an obvious news point, or if it has one, you may be loath to use it because it's not in itself frantically interesting. Here's an example: a woman retires as chair of a local council, a post she has held for 10 years. She makes a speech, talks about the memorable events that took place during her time in charge, and is given a leaving gift. It's the sort of story often found in local newspapers, company newsletters, etc. So far, so unremarkable. You could use it to write something along the following lines:

> After 10 years heading Brentfield Council, Barbara Suit spoke to friends and colleagues before they presented her with garden tools as a retirement present.

This is completely factual and functional, and clocks in at 24 words, but it hardly encourages you to read the rest of the story. So what would? Try this:

> As Brentfield Council boss Barbara Suit quit after 10 years, she revealed that ending free school bus travel was the toughest decision she took.

This is shorter, and has a different news point. It still takes the woman's retirement as its starting point, but has lifted something from what she said, about a decision that could very well have had a direct impact on a person reading the story, or people close to him or her, and in the process reveals something he or she probably did not know before.

Wanting to find out things is part of human nature, as is discovering what makes people tick, so the story now has a more personal hook to draw in readers. Someone revealing the hardest decision they've taken at work is potentially interesting. Giving a retiring council official a shovel and some other horticultural paraphernalia is interesting only to the receiver of these items.

Is this sensationalising a straightforward story? I don't think so. Instead, a little lateral thinking is being applied as to the best way of employing the information at the writer's disposal, seeing the merit in facts which are not the most instantly obvious ones and using them accordingly. In a very basic way, this comes under the heading of research. It also means taking the writer's mind off autopilot when putting the story together, which makes it more interesting to do. If you feel disengaged from a subject, this will show in your words.

'Newspaper and magazine editors cut material from the bottom, working on the principle that the least important facts will be at the end.'

Although there are no absolute rules for how the rest of the item should be written, getting a direct quote from the person involved as the second or third paragraph provides confirmation of what was said at the top of the story. So, you'd have something like this:

> As Brentfield Council boss Barbara Suit quit after 10 years, she revealed that ending free school bus travel was the toughest decision she took.
>
> 'I knew how difficult it would be for some people, but rising fuel costs meant that in the end we had to find additional ways of paying for the service or risk losing it completely. Of all the choices I had to take, this was the hardest,' said Suit, 56, who announced her retirement earlier this year, saying it was time for a younger person to take over.

Speaking at a ceremony to mark her retirement from the authority's top job, the outgoing council leader talked about the highs and lows of making decisions that affected the lives of thousands of local people. She counted the school bus saga and ongoing vandalism among the latter, but said that securing government money to rebuild the 1920s' Paxton cinema and improving amenities for the elderly were among the things she was most proud of achieving.

Colleagues paid tribute to the councillor, who has plans for a busy retirement. Her leaving present, a set of garden tools, gave a strong hint about how she will be spending her time.

This certainly isn't earth-shattering stuff, but it does extract a good quantity of human interest from what is a fairly dry story, and although it's short and does not provide a résumé of its subject's career, it tells you that she's retiring, reveals something new about her work (the school bus crisis) and says why she's leaving, then fleshes out elements of her career. The garden tools reference is used as a light pay-off at the end. If lack of space means the item has to be shortened, it's a piece of information that's easily cut. As a rule of thumb, newspaper and magazine editors cut material from the bottom, working on the principle that the least important facts will be at the end. Whatever you're writing, ordering it as if this is the case will give it structure.

> 'As a rule of thumb, newspaper and magazine editors cut material from the bottom.'

English as she is writ

It's easy to derail a story's meaning by getting the order of facts knotted up or with an unfortunate piece of punctuation – putting a full stop or comma in the wrong place or leaving them out altogether. Here's an example dug up from a local newspaper:

> A concerned resident has reiterated her claims that the town is growing increasingly dirty, spurred on by support from her last appeal.

Have a little think about what this sentence really says. Its meaning is clear enough, but what's been written actually implies that the rise in dirtiness has been 'spurred on by support from her last appeal'. It's OK, but a bit sloppy. Had the writer come up with something along the lines of: 'A concerned resident says her claim that the town is growing increasingly dirty has been backed up by local people, spurred on by her last appeal,' then things would be clear. This sentence is hardly an example of Shakespearian elegance, but it's now less fuddled.

However, read on and you realise that this isn't actually what the story is about, despite a headline that read, 'Clean-up campaign gathers support'. The dirt-busting lady ran a shop, complained that the streets near it were getting muckier – which is a personal opinion or a complaint, not a campaign – and this caused another local trader to say that they weren't dirty at all. The 'campaign' story was her response to his comments.

Given this, an opening sentence that read, 'Local business woman Muriel Doily [note: this name is an invented one] has hit back at claims that her description of the town as "filthy" is untrue.' would be much clearer.

As written, the original item was nine paragraphs long, but the comments that sparked it didn't appear until the penultimate one. They should have been near the top of the story, so you would have something along the lines of:

> Local businesswoman Muriel Doily has hit back at claims that her description of the town as 'filthy' is untrue.
> 'When I look out of my shop front I don't see too many

problems,' shop owner Dave Jockstrap told *The Weekly Bugler* [two more fake names, gentle reader] on March 2nd, 'I can't agree with her totally. How fastidious do you need to be?'

Mrs Doily, owner of the Bun in the Oven tea rooms, said Mr Jockstrap needed to look further than his business frontage, 'and keep his eyes open'. She added that many locals had backed her claims. 'It's been amazing. I've had wonderful support,' she said. The tea room owner said the town's recreation ground was still blighted by discarded fast food cartons, and that she regularly saw one elderly man clearing litter from his hedge, but Mr Jockstrap remains unconvinced. 'I don't think it's anything to worry about,' he said.

> **'As with many stories, the news point here can be simply that someone has expressed an opinion.'**

To get the same information over in the original story's latter half, its writer had resorted to using direct quotes from the opposing camps. This is a good way to attribute facts and opinions to identifiable, and hopefully reputable, sources, because it's not the story's author saying something is happening.

As with many stories, the news point here can be simply that someone has expressed an opinion. Provided it isn't a deliberate lie or defamatory, this is newsworthy in itself. However, spoken English does not always translate easily onto the page. It can play havoc with grammar. Words that are used incorrectly when spoken often barely register to a listener, but will jump out at him or her when written down, as will the repetition of words and phrases.

I think the quotes as used in the original town clean-up item demonstrate this and also smack a little of filling space. With a few name changes, this is what was written:

She said: 'Grotville-on-Sea doesn't start and finish at the front of his shop. He needs to go around Grotville and keep his eyes open.

'I have had so many people come up to me and say, "Well done, it's time someone spoke up about the filth."

'It's been amazing. I have had wonderful support.'

She added: 'I see it every day. People buy fast food and throw the rubbish on the recreation ground.

'When I go to St. Brian's church market every week I see an elderly gentleman clearing up the rubbish under his hedge along the road into town.'

Mr Jockstrap said: 'I can't agree with her totally. I live in Grotville-on-Sea and I don't see too many problems. When I look out my shop front I don't see too many problems. How fastidious have you got to be?

'I don't think it's anything to worry about.'

Quite a lot of words have been used here to say a relatively small amount, and the second-to-last paragraph is grammatically suspect ('When I look out my shop' – Mr J. really should have been looking out of his shop). The quote goes on to say the same thing twice in consecutive sentences: that the man does not see 'too many problems' in the town, and again that he does not see 'too many problems' from his shop.

It would be a much better idea to take these two statements out of direct quotation, and combine them into a sentence attributed to him, but where the repetition can be killed off ('Mr Jockstrap said that he didn't see a lot of rubbish in the town or near his shop'). This will leave the writer needing more fresh, quotable information, but this shouldn't be a hardship. Going back and asking Mrs Doily if she hoped her comments would spark a clean-up campaign would probably do it, and whether she said 'yes' or 'no', her answer could provide the follow-up story.

Opinion formers

One problem, which sometimes seems endemic when it comes to writing about newsworthy events, is that the author's opinions creep into the copy, and are presented as facts. Actually, they may very well be factual, but a degree of distance is necessary, and the more emotive the subject, the more important that distance becomes.

If something is added to a story because you think it is so, it becomes comment, not fact, and comment can get you into trouble, and blur the boundaries of the story itself. For instance, you could be writing a story about a particularly contentious planning application, for a building that would radically change the character of the area for which it is intended.

> **'If something is added to a story because you think it is so, it becomes comment, not fact.'**

You may have a personal interest in, or feel incensed by, these events, and have justification for your anger, but your feelings are not the story. So, if you were to write, 'Local residents of an unspoiled village street will see the character of their homes ruined by an ugly development of flats,' you might be spot on, but this is still personal opinion. The developer might claim that his proposed flats are in fact very attractive, and that what you have written is malicious. This would be hard to prove one way or the other, especially if the buildings are only at the planning stage. A set of drawings is often innocuous, but there are plenty of solicitors who would be only too happy to extract money from the builder and despatch an official letter warning of the dire consequences to their client's business and reputation created by what you have written.

You just try proving that his double-glazed condominiums aren't entirely charming. One person's brutal box is another's modernist dream. On a personal level, you are absolutely entitled to say that you think they would be an eyesore, and give reasons why this is so, if you have been asked to write a comment piece, provided you stick to the specifics and don't engage in personal attacks that cannot be substantiated. Why? Because this would be a subjective story. However, get somebody else with a vested interest or expertise to say what they think about the buildings, and if their words tally with the thing that you think appears self-evident, it can be woven into the text. The story itself is that they, rather than you, have said it.

So, a person whose home would be next door to the flats might say that he thinks they're too big or out of keeping with the surrounding properties. If he's not accusing the developer of bestial acts with reptiles (because of a sense of personal enmity), and he does not make obviously daft or inaccurate claims, then his opinion is newsworthy, since he has a direct, personal interest in what is being proposed. As a result, you could write a story that began, 'Plans to build flats in an ancient village have been branded ill-conceived by a resident whose home will be overlooked by them.'

> **'It is not up to the writer of a story to slant it so that one or other party is damned – let them hang themselves.'**

You would then follow this up with a direct, attributable quote from the person concerned, expressing what he thinks about the proposals, and why he is against them. Subsequent paragraphs should provide hard information on what will be built, where, how much, etc., and there should also be quotes from the developers. It's vital to give them the right of reply. Their views are as important as the view of the person with which you are leading the piece. The developers' views provide balance, and allow readers to make up their own minds about what is being claimed by both sides.

Again, your personal judgement on the merits of these arguments really ought to take a back seat. If one party is clearly wrong, then that should become obvious in factual terms and by what they say. It is not up to the writer of a story to slant it so that one or other party is damned – let them hang themselves. By being accurate and fair to everyone involved, the justice, or otherwise, of all the claims being made will emerge.

Truth or dare?

I'm not saying deliberate slanting of stories doesn't happen. Quite the reverse. Scratch the surface of a lot of journalism, especially if it concerns a subject that you are familiar with, and you'll often find that it follows a particular editorial line, sometimes at the expense of the piece itself. I once worked for a trade newspaper editor who said, 'Never let the facts get in the way of a good story.' This was said in jest, but judging by what he allowed onto the page, the man was only half joking.

Actually, it's the facts themselves that make a good story, and having an open mind will allow you to write fairly about them. In this case, you might find that the person who now vociferously objects to the plans once supported them, and tried to sell the developer a piece of his garden for an inflated price. When the sale didn't go through he then switched sides.

If something like this is said, it's important to go back to the original source and ask him about it. He might flatly deny what has been claimed, and this should go into your piece. Equally, he might say that he was always against the development in principle, was asked to sell and sent the developer packing, or investigated the garden sale but was offered an insufficient amount of money. None of these things necessarily change the piece's original news point, but they would be relevant, and really ought to be part of what you write.

Critical detachment is a very good thing to have while in the process of stitching together opposing opinions into a story – deciding which part of it is the most important and should therefore become its news point – rather than making a decision about this before you have researched. Often you will know what the likely news point is from the beginning, but refusing to change it if the information does not fit is a mistake sometimes made by journalists.

My personal career nemesis came when a long-departed trade press news editor of a bi-monthly magazine instructed me to look at a local government-related story from a rival publication. This was a slapdash item with no clear news point, as the first paragraph said that two virtually unrelated things had happened to an official body a fortnight previously. Where was the news in this? It was my job to find out, or so I thought.

I made some phone calls, discovered how things had moved on since, chose one of the subjects to lead my piece, and since there was a slight connection between the things originally described, worked in developments about the second fact towards the end of my story.

> **'Often the divide between fact and opinion is hard to gauge, but if you can't back something up, don't put it in.'**

My boss was not pleased. He'd told me to rewrite, not update, and when I was silly enough to argue that the original story was vague beyond endurance, and almost inaccurate as a result, he fixed me with a particularly fishy stare and said, 'What you have written is inaccurate too. You have used the word "or" instead of "nor".' An easily changed grammatical error meant more to him than what the piece actually said. That I was being asked to plagiarize a rotten story also seemed to have passed him by.

Speculate to decimate

This magazine also encouraged its writers to add personal speculation into their news pieces, often expressed as hard fact, and not actually attributed to anyone. As a practice this went completely against the training its publishers gave to their journalists, and potentially was also a great way to land its staff in court.

'Well, your honour, I thought that the council's restructuring would lead to massive job losses so that's what I wrote, and, um, then they didn't – but I don't see how they can claim that my article caused their staff any unnecessary distress.'

Often the divide between fact and opinion is hard to gauge, but if you can't back something up, don't put it in.

Be sure

Making sure you understand all the elements of your story fully is also vitally important. Assuming that something is so, without making certain, isn't good enough. If you're unsure, check and re-check. This may mean phoning people several times to corroborate the most apparently banal details.

> **'Is the person who's the source of your story really in the know?'**

I wrote a story about vehicle insurance and made the assumption that a body quoted in it looked after the interests of insurance brokers. Strictly speaking, this wasn't correct; they had a wider remit, and kicked up a fuss that went on for weeks. They tried to imply that calling them 'an insurance brokers' body' was damaging to their reputation. Frankly, this was trying it on. Letters were written in the hope that the newspaper might give them some money to go away. Eventually they did go away, empty handed, but this was a self-inflicted misfortune for me. I had been sloppy and careless, and the problems this created did not make me popular with the commissioning editor, who had to deal with the result.

So leaving nothing to chance is also important. Are the figures you've used correct? Is the person who's the source of your story really in the know? If you take what they've said as gospel and use it without attribution, it's your words that will appear wrong.

When working as a commissioning editor, I was given a complex story about car tax. It was written by a freelance journalist and didn't ring true, so I asked for a rewrite. When the piece's premise still seemed suspect, I asked the author to clarify the information and identify its source. This turned out to be a consultant who valued second-hand cars, with whom the journalist had been speaking about something else. What the consultant had said was off the cuff and wrong. The journalist should have checked with the relevant taxation authorities but didn't, and instead vamped up an ill-informed comment into a story.

Another colleague got his knuckles wrapped for lifting entire quotes and paragraphs of data from newspapers without attributing their original sources. This came to light when one of his 'borrowings' turned out to be incorrect. Up to a point, it's perfectly OK to quote from almost any published medium, provided you credit it with being the source ('according to the *London Times*, 20 breeding pairs of peregrine falcons have been released into the wild'). This is attribution. Taking the information as if it's something you've unearthed ('twenty pairs of peregrine falcons have been released into the wild') is theft. Also, stories of this sort ought to be backed up with information you've found for yourself.

> **'Up to a point, it's perfectly OK to quote from almost any published medium, provided you credit it with being the source.'**

What's in a name?

Let's get back to accuracy. Have you got everyone's job or official titles right? Some are so meaningless in the abstract that it pays to ask for a brief description of what they mean and paraphrase this, rather than using some wordy 'assistant chief facilitator (logistics)' style title, which might baffle your readers. You might find the person with this endless title is a distribution manager.

Treat brand and product names with care. Some names, like Hoover, have taken on meanings never imagined by their promoters. In many parts of the world the term 'to hoover' means to vacuum clean, and although its copyright remains with the makers of Hoover-branded electrical products, its generic use means the name is often applied as a verb to describe using rival cleaners.

This sort of thing makes trade mark owners very keen to keep control of their famous – or less famous – names, and defend their copyrights. According to journalism trainer Richard Sharpe, these copyrights are renewed every 10 years in Britain, and their owners have to prove that they've been defended against 'inappropriate' use, which is why solicitors are kept gainfully employed sending official letters to people writing for the most obscure titles. For instance, Portakabin, which amongst other things makes temporary buildings, is sometimes moved to express displeasure with writers who've described these structures as 'portakabins', (note the lower case 'p') when they might have been made by someone else, or the name has been used as a generic description.

> **'Don't assume that because you've seen a famous name half a million times that you'll spell it properly.'**

Likewise, Levi's, the clothing manufacturer famous for its jeans, takes a dim view of anybody using their name without the apostrophe. Write about 'Xeroxing' rather than photocopying, and you could incur the displeasure of Xerox, the office equipment manufacturer, which owns that name and wants to keep control over how it's applied.

Some businesses appear completely neurotic about how their trademarked names are used (although I wouldn't dare to suggest that this applies to Hoover, Portakabin, Levi's or Xerox, m'lud), and their complaints can seem spurious – sometimes they are – but this is something worth bearing in mind, especially when it comes to checking spellings used in your writing. Brand names can sometimes employ odd uses of capital letters (BMW makes a car called the Mini, but irritatingly, calls it the MINI – all those capitals stand out on the page) and punctuation marks. Don't assume that because you've seen a famous name half a million times that you'll spell it properly. Familiarity breeds carelessness, so check.

Are interviewees' names spelt correctly? If in doubt, ask. The normal social processes of not wanting to bother people have to be put aside. The minor irritation somebody might feel because you've phoned them two or three times to get seemingly uninspiring details right will be as nothing compared to the anger they are likely to feel if your words are wrong.

I interviewed a man with quite sibilant speech, and took down his surname as 'Wetton', when in fact it was 'Welton'. This was picked up before the story went out, but the person who noticed the error had a personal interest in the subject, and was quick to express his displeasure at having to go right through my copy and correct it. I should have asked the man to spell his name.

> **'Before committing yourself utterly to a story, it's worth checking it through one last time.'**

There can be very good reasons why mistakes creep into written work. An author can be tired, stressed, working to tight deadlines, or briefly distracted, but the bottom line is that those mistakes are his or her responsibility, and nobody else's. Before committing yourself utterly to a story, it's worth checking it through one last time. The time spent doing so can often save a lot of grief in the long term.

Since we're in confessional mode, I once wrote a story that I thought was spot on, but turned out to be anything but. It was about importing

American cars into Europe – which was a complicated and involved process – and was being produced for a newspaper that had not previously taken my work. Having discussed what would go in it and the order this information would run, and been asked to produce some specific costings, I managed to get these wrong. Also, some of the information was not in the order requested.

Rather than chuck it back and ask me to make the necessary corrections, the commissioning editor rewrote everything bar two paragraphs, and I have not worked for him since. Such things are far too easily done if you do not think hard and concentrate on what you have written.

Does it really say what you intended it to? Don't assume that this is the case. Whether you're writing something that will only be seen by friends and neighbours or a piece for a national newspaper or magazine, it's your name that will be attached to it.

Don't take flight

If your words are intended for publication, it's common practice for questions to be asked about them by the editors and sub-editors you are writing for, and even if the answers to those questions seem blindingly obvious to you, giving the right answers should be part of what you do. Editors should also get you to question whether your work is as clear as you'd thought. Others can pick up on things that you may miss.

'Should there be an error, and it's your fault, own up.'

Should there be an error, and it's your fault, own up – there's no need to grovel, but taking responsibility for something and apologising is usually the best way to minimise the fallout it's created. If things go wrong, try to look honestly at why, rather than feeling defensive and embarrassed. Applying critical detachment to getting something wrong is hard to do, because mistakes make one feel awkward and uncomfortable, but it's worthwhile, because this will allow you to avoid repeating them.

The causes might not be directly your fault. The source of a story could be misinformed, or have given you a bum steer, in which case you'll know not to use them again, or if you do, to treat what they say with particular caution. Once again, taking a hard look at what led to an error will assist you in the long term.

Aircraft engineers have a very similar approach to what they do. Lives depend on their work being spot-on, so if someone drops a spanner into the wing of a passenger plane, they don't keep quiet, even if retrieving it will take hours and wreck the airline's schedule, because the plane can't be used safely. Approach your mistakes in the same way and this will ultimately enhance your credibility and keep you out of trouble.

Take note

Having clear, easily accessed notes is also a must. If you're quoting someone directly ('I sold the house because it was mine,' said the actress's ex-husband), those quotes need to be demonstrably what they said, and that means having the information on paper. If they come back to you and claim to have been misquoted, you can refer to your notes. Equally, facts and figures can sometimes be disputed. Having them in easily accessed written form should cover you in a dispute.

> **'Not keeping reasonably ordered, comprehensible notes is career suicide for anyone with professional writing aspirations.'**

There are fairly abstruse legal requirements attached to taking notes and storing information, but not keeping reasonably ordered, comprehensible notes is career suicide for anyone with professional writing aspirations, and bad practice for others whose words will be read by other people, even at a very local level. I'd recommend keeping such material for at least three years.

Practical applications

A great many of the organisational, ethical and practical things we've looked at in the context of writing news stories should be applied to other forms of writing (as we shall see in the following chapter about feature stories, which are generally less prescriptive in content and format).

Well written news journalism leaves little room for individual writing style, because ultimately it's what a story says rather than how it says it that is the most important thing. This is writing to a formula, but once you've grasped it, making that formula work for you, developing angles, researching and producing a tightly written piece, can be immensely satisfying, because 300 words about a factory strike can be as well crafted as 3,000 on something more personal.

- Make your opening sentence 25–35 words long. It should tell the reader what the rest of the story is about.

- The word 'news' is derived from 'new'. Your story needs to be about something new, or a new development of an existing event. If it's old, it's not news.

- What's the point of your story? Could you explain this succinctly? If not, work this out before you start writing.

- A story's 'news point' can be an event or a statement. In the latter instance, it's newsworthy because of who said it, what they said, or why they said it. Reactions to it are also news.

- What are the most important elements of the item you're writing? They should appear in descending order of importance.

- If a story's subject involves differing opinions, flag them up. This will give it balance.

- Your personal opinion is not newsworthy, even if you're right. Keep bias out of your story and allow the facts to speak for themselves.

- Check facts, quotes, spellings and acronyms. If you're unsure of your ground, re-check, and assume nothing.

Chapter 4

THE BASICS, PART 2
Feature writing – essays for grown-ups

If you've just read the last chapter about news writing,
you might well think it prescriptive, not to say restrictive,
and fall upon this one with a glad cry. Feature writing
certainly gives you more space, and to some extent
more freedom over what you write and how you
write it. The disadvantage of this is that
you can be confronted with the hell
of acres of white space to fill.

In the abstract, this might be seen as a writerly opportunity to expand
ideas and describe things with wit and elegance, but anyone who has
been given a 2,000-word slot to fill, and finds they only have 1,000
words' worth of things to say, will be familiar with the uncomfortable,
clammy feeling of being caught short (in a literary sense).

There is some blurring between writing that can be described as
news-driven, and feature material. You can have a long news story of
about 500 words, but the same length would also make a short feature.
News-related items of this length or over, which take the contents of a
story and examine them in more depth, looking at why something has
happened and its likely impact in the longer term, are often described
as analysis or overview pieces.

Often they will be less time-sensitive than a pure news piece, and
will have involved digging out facts and commentary to amplify ideas

and arguments that a hard news item might not have space to include.

Another area where there can be some crossover between news and features is comment. Everybody has an opinion about something, and some of us are asked to put this onto the printed page. Comment stories can range from an expert's view of a given subject, where an argument is presented from a factual viewpoint, to subjective words on whatever exercises the writer's mind. Here the potential subject material is endless, from reviewing an amateur play, or indeed any art form, to explaining why Britney Spears is the most talented singer the western world has produced since Maria Callas. Such things are personal opinions, personally expressed, and have little to do with news journalism – unless you're a person of note, and somebody else decides what you've said is newsworthy ('"Britney beats Callas" says top writer').

> **'You can be confronted with the hell of acres of white space to fill.'**

There are some writers who've made a very good living as 'name' columnists churning out this stuff. You might look with envy at the platforms they've been given on which to pontificate, but having something to say once a week – or even once a month – can prove hard to maintain, which is why you'll find a lot of inconsequential fluff and over-egged rants about nothing very much, where expressing an opinion has slipped into posturing. In truth, the writer often has nothing to say, but has to come up with something to fill the space.

The market for this sort of thing is a limited and generally rather exclusive one, populated by experts, public figures or well connected professional pundits. Trying to sell a column idea to a publication – particularly one whose editors haven't come across you – is virtually impossible. So let us concentrate on feature writing in the form of producing words on an event or a happening. Again, the best place to start is with the intro or opening paragraph.

Opening shots

Unlike news writing, where you are tied down to a formula, with a feature there's room for a bit more creativity in what is written, or how you write it. However, you do need a hook (in other words an idea) to draw the reader in to the rest of the piece. Knocking out something which is baldly factual often isn't enough.

Suppose you have to produce some words on farm cider making, and kick off the piece with:

> Farmer Barry Wells expects to use 10 tons of apples for his cider production this year, three tons more than the year before.

Well gosh. This gives you the facts, but it's functional to the point of joylessness. Unless you're a cider obsessive or an apple junkie, is there anything in these words to make you want to keep reading? No? Well, there ought to be, and you can afford to have a little fun here, so how about:

> For farmer Barry Wells 'Double Vision' isn't a medical problem, it's a drink.

This intro is slightly jokey, and should get your reader to ask, 'Why is it called "Double Vision"? What sort of drink is it?' Reading more of the story will supply the answers. You are drawing the person in, rather than making an assumption that their interest will be aroused by some bland statistics.

'**You do need a hook (in other words an idea) to draw the reader in to the rest of the piece.**'

You can use the stuff about how many apples the farmer uses in the subsequent paragraph, and, without labouring the point too much, it might be possible to drop in another reference to the cider's focus-altering brand name when doing so. One paragraph could read,

Wells uses his apple crop to make cider, and expects to use an extra three tons of fruit to meet demand for his prophetically named brew.

There's an obvious human interest element to this piece. Person makes his own drink and other people buy it. Generating an intro on the back of this ought to be relatively straightforward; however, the interesting or unusual elements of some stories can be harder to pin down when looking for a good peg on which to hang an intro. This does not mean that you should not try to find them.

First person

Quotes often make excellent intros, but generally you should resist the temptation to use them in this way, because the quotation marks tend to look awkward, especially when a bigger, 'drop cap' capital letter is used for the first word – a common feature of many newspaper and magazine design layouts, viz.:

'One day the world will come to know the genius of vampire bats,' reckons animal behaviourist Dr Helen Schwarz, who has studied Count Dracula's pet of choice.

This can often look awkward on the page, and the best way around the problem is to incorporate or paraphrase the quote into your opening paragraph, so that it doesn't start with inverted commas or speech marks:

It wasn't Count Dracula who said, 'One day the world will come to know the genius of vampire bats.' That honour goes to animal behaviourist Dr Helen Schwarz, who has studied them closely.

Another way around this is to take the meat of the quote and paraphrase it so that the meaning remains, but the quotation marks do not, like this:

For wildlife genius, animal behaviourist Dr Helen Schwarz thinks the vampire bat should be your creature of choice.

The permutations are almost endless, and if the person quoted has a lot of interesting things to say, and what you are writing is not just a straight interview, they can be spread liberally through your story. On the other hand, if the way the person expresses themselves is laboured or inarticulate, but the meaning of what he or she says is clear enough, you can rewrite or tighten up their words so that it becomes your writing but with the sense of what it contains attributed to the person who gave you the information.

Never a dull moment

Assuming that some subjects are so dry, obscure or dull, that less exacting standards can apply to the way they're written about is creative and professional death. Lower your standards and readers will be turned off by what you have written. Do you really want your name against something which is mediocre? If you're a half decent writer this should never happen, and good words can turn up in some very obscure places.

For instance, Christian Wolmar, the campaigning British transport journalist, who has worked for newspapers such as *The Independent*, writes extensively for railway magazines aimed, you would think, at men whose interest is primarily railway engine numbers.

> **'Lower your standards and readers will be turned off by what you have written.'**

Nevertheless, his words in these magazines are every bit as trenchant and finely tuned as his national press output.

You might not have read *Diesel Car* magazine lately, but Sue Baker, one of its contributors, was *The Observer*'s motoring correspondent, and is a regular freelance contributor to the UK nationals and *SAGA*

Magazine. Baker applies the same standards to all these outlets as *Diesel Car*. She understands that you're only as good as the last thing you wrote, even if it's a few hundred words tucked away in the back of a trade magazine. The quality of those words is your calling card. It's surprising the number of professional writers who drop their standards for low profile work, or deride it as 'boring'. They're treating both the readers and the people who have commissioned them with contempt, which is a bad career move.

> 'Start from the premise that what you're writing is dull or unimportant, then this will show in the way the end product reads.'

If you have no journalistic ambitions, but are reading this in the hope that it will help improve your day-to-day writing, you might very well say 'so what?' Well, there is a connection. Start from the premise that what you're writing is dull or unimportant, then this will show in the way the end product reads. Your writing will inevitably have a perfunctory, join-the-dots quality. It will probably be harder to get the words onto the page as well. Deciding a subject is banal means that time spent producing words about it will drag, as your mind wanders off to all the more interesting things you could be doing.

> 'There's no such thing as a boring story, only boring journalists.'

Once, while working as a reporter for a trade magazine aimed at personnel officers (or 'human resources managers' as they like to be known), I was grinding through a story about training. Everybody I spoke to seemed to be a person in a suit called Brian, who repeated the mantra, 'we need more training'. One day I complained bitterly that the subject was entirely interest-free.

'There's no such thing as a boring story,' said the features editor, 'only boring journalists.'

She was right. No matter what you're writing, finding interest in it, or a fresh way to express a familiar thought, subject or idea is always possible, and will make the process of putting these things down on paper less of a drudge.

Too exciting

It's true that some subjects are, shall we say, more engaging than others. I once spent three days dashing across Italy following a classic car road race called the Mille Miglia, which involved fabulous Bentleys, Alfa Romeos, Ferraris and Bugattis charging through beautiful Italian countryside and congregating in places like Sienna, Verona and St Mark's Square. This was a riotous experience and a joy to write about.

The words for my road race story came rather more easily than the piece I'd previously been commissioned to produce for a staff magazine, on a new sports club building a large chemical company had opened for its staff. Located in an outer London suburb, the place was hardly thrill-a-minute stuff on paper, but then I spoke to the architect. He talked enthusiastically about why the building had ended up looking the way it did, which had something to do with the shape of the land (it had to be squeezed into a space between a busy road, railway line and a playing field). He discussed making it accessible to disabled employees, why he'd chosen certain materials for the furnishings in the reception area, and even the lighting used there, to create a particular ambience. This was an insider's knowledge, which brought interest to a familiar environment, explaining why it looked the way it did.

This could have been a rather arid story that started along the lines of, 'Staff at DullCorp International plc can take advantage of squash courts and a bowling alley at the company's new purpose-built sports facility,' followed by a sort of shopping list of the building's features. Instead, we had a story along the lines of:

> Chrome and strip lights have been banned at DullCorp's just-opened sports complex. 'We wanted to create the feel of an airline's executive waiting room rather than a gym,' said architect Ben Setsquare, explaining why the facility's reception area is lit with halogen lamps, and makes extensive use of maple wood for its wall cladding and furnishings. 'The reception room is long, with curving walls, and quite narrow at one end, and we felt that a pale wood could be used to follow its shape, make the space feel less impersonal and reduce the echo you get from stone walls.'

I could then bring in stuff about how the choice of lighting meant that the environment didn't have the ambience of a railway station waiting room, and helped make it more inviting, before launching into a detailed account of what the place actually contained.

A little historical digging revealed that the company had owned the land on which it had been built since the 1930s, and had used it to provide staff with leisure facilities in the decades since, so that gave me some historical context and nice background material. The end result wasn't going to rival a Harry Potter novel for interest and excitement, but as a story it went beyond bald facts, brought in quotes from real people who had been involved in making something, and lifted the piece from propaganda into something that had been genuinely engaging to research.

It didn't beat watching a 1920s' Alfa Romeo worth more than my house snake down a sun-drenched Italian mountain pass, but finding interest in the sports club story, and presenting it to other people, had its own satisfaction.

On another occasion, I had to write about a car dealer that had built a new showroom. This was a modern, pre-stressed structure made from a bolted together metal frame and large sheets of glass. Anyone who has read local newspaper stories about this sort of thing will almost be able to picture the kind of sentence this might create.

Leading luxury car dealer Clive's of Dunville celebrated the opening of its all-new, purpose-built, high tech showroom with a champagne reception for invited guests and customers, and promised the facility would provide an exciting, customer-focused sales environment.

Yes, this was a new industrial unit building with cars in it, and that's the sort of cliché-laden paragraph that betrays the author's bafflement at what to say about it, and a join-the-dots mindset about the things that made it interesting. In order to keep an impending sense of suicidal boredom at bay I concentrated on the way the building had been made, and came up with something like:

Builders needed spanners rather than trowels and cement when they set about creating Clive's of Dunville's latest showroom.

The idea behind this was that it would make people think, 'Why? What's it made of?' and hopefully persuade them to go on to read all the practical nuts and bolts stuff – pardon the pun – about what the building contained and why. Once again, I needed a hook, which thankfully the building's construction provided.

A similar mindset can be applied to almost any form of writing, whether it's reporting on a piece of amateur dramatics, or

> 'Approach anything you have to write about with an open mind, and you'll be surprised how much easier it is to produce the words.'

knocking out a few hundred words for a parish magazine on clearing rubbish from a village pond. Somebody might have used a long-forgotten family heirloom like a wind-up record player to dress the play's set, or peculiar things might have been dredged from that pond (like 15 pairs of shoes – which raises some questions, viz. how did they get in there? Did their owners go home with bare feet?). Very often interest can be found in an event's detail, rather than the event itself, and uncovering that detail, by asking questions and being prepared to follow tangents, can create something that's more interesting to write and read.

So, approach anything you have to write about with an open mind, and you'll be surprised how much easier it is to produce the words.

Curb your enthusiasm – a bit

Of course enthusiasm for a subject can be a wonderful thing. It can enliven how you write, and help bring your words to life. Also, being able to add expertise to a feature has the potential to lift and bring credibility to it. The best specialist writing thrives on this. Whether the words are about rock music or plastic bottle making, a mix of insider knowledge and interest in the subject can open it up for others, but as ever, there are pitfalls to be avoided.

'Your prime loyalty really should be those reading your words, not the providers of their subject matter.'

In the chapter relating to news stories, I ranted on about how writers should never regard their opinions as newsworthy in themselves. With feature stories that aren't strictly observational or personal (so, not things like travel stories or restaurant reviews), the writer also ought to aim for some critical detachment from the subject, and not perceive him or herself as speaking on its behalf.

This happens frequently in many areas of journalism. Product journalism is a good example, where items usually produced by a fairly limited number of companies are written about by a fairly limited number of writers. Often fruitful working and sometimes personal relationships are developed with journalists and public relations people, product experts, designers, and so on. Favoured writers can be offered exclusive interviews and stories that sometimes involve travel and access to products the public won't see for months or years.

If your personal enthusiasm is for fashion, cameras or sailing ships, and your job provides access to the top people or products in these fields, you would hardly be human if you weren't excited at the prospect. However, your prime loyalty really should be to those reading your words, not the providers of their subject matter.

'Too many journalists soft-pedal on stories, for fear of upsetting contacts or their "friends" in the industry.'

I know of one hard-working and extremely nice motoring writer who produced a laudatory story about a car maker, which actually tried to present a fall in sales as a positive development. Within a year of his writing it, the company went belly-up.

Believe it or not, this man wasn't being wilfully dishonest, but ethically he'd lost his bearings. I think he genuinely wanted to help his car making pals by showing them in a good light, and 'do his bit' to promote their once-great company, whose name and products had been an important part of his life since childhood. In the process, he'd forgotten about the needs of his readers, who might have read his words and bought cars from a manufacturer that would soon cease to exist. This did nothing for his credibility as an independent writer.

Too many journalists soft-pedal on stories, for fear of upsetting contacts or their 'friends' in the industry. They worry that the supply of stories and 'perks' will be cut off, or that they'll be blamed for causing something to fail because they didn't write about it in a positive way. Peer pressure can be a powerful force.

Most people who work in public relations aren't evil manipulators, they're just men and women earning a living, but it is their job to be on friendly terms with writers and supply them with positive information or deal with, and if possible neutralise, unhelpful stories, perhaps by putting a positive spin on them.

As a writer, it's sometimes perfectly OK to take a spoonfed item from a source like this, so long as it's interesting in journalistic terms, accurate, and has not been presented as part of some broader, hidden agenda. Also, if such an idea can be taken forward and developed by a writer, it shouldn't be dismissed.

I spent several entertaining but rather hair-raising days using an old American hot rod car as my everyday transport, and wrote about this for a newspaper. The hot rod was owned by a business that specialised in supplying spare parts for old American vehicles. They'd taken on a freelance public relations man, who came up with the idea, knew that I wrote slightly left-field pieces, and offered this one to me. My story mentioned where the car had been supplied from, and said what the company did, but didn't focus on this. Since the hot rod was unique, this seemed like a fair exchange.

However, I did once write an ill-timed business feature about a car manufacturer that had made a success of selling its wares through small, often family-owned dealerships, which was published just weeks before the company sacked a lot of them. I wrote about that too, and there wasn't a murmur of complaint from the manufacturer's publicity people. However, shortly afterwards they offered me a story on how rally cars sponsored by its dealers were being used to train young drivers, and had proved useful in generating local newspaper coverage for dealers when the rally cars visited them.

I duly turned round another business feature, for the same publication that had taken my previous two stories. It appeared and rather eclipsed the 'sacked dealers' item. Had I been manipulated? Absolutely, but this might equally be seen as the publicity person doing her job properly, by getting a writer to follow up a decent enough story with a positive spin rather than shouting at him over one which did not show her company in a good light. You can apply similar strictures with news stories.

I've talked a lot about car journalism here because, up to a point, it's a subject I know something about, but you can apply a similar yardstick to a great deal of specialist features, or product-based stories.

What are you on about?

If you know something about a subject, it's also very easy to ghettoise it by writing as if the reader is also an expert. Using specialist terms without explaining what they mean is a prime example. People who do this are sometimes guilty of writing to impress their peers by showing how much they know. There's a slightly tribal 'we're the in crowd, because we know stuff you don't' element to this sort of thing, which can be found everywhere from book reviews to magazines about dog breeding.

> **'Whatever you're writing, pitch it so that lay people and experts alike can make sense of it.'**

Unless you're writing for an audience that wants and expects highly specific information in a specialist journal, all you are doing is excluding readers who might potentially be interested in a given subject. Never assume knowledge, or write in a way that implies you think the person who sees your story *should* know what you mean. There was a time when you didn't know either, and taking a few words to explain a process or spell out an acronym, will help open it up to them.

For example, in motoring writing the term 'ABS' is often used. This stands for 'Anti-lock Braking System', but if this isn't spelt out the first time it's written (e.g. 'ABS (Anti-lock Braking System)', or 'Anti-lock Braking System (ABS)'), the term will remain a mystery to some people. Once explained, it can be used throughout your story. This is a generic piece of good practice whatever your subject matter.

Of course, if you want to produce marginalising, obscure and self-indulgent work, ignore what I've just said.

Whatever you're writing, pitch it so that lay people and experts alike can make sense of it. You shouldn't produce copy to show off or lecture. Quality and wit ought to shine from your words, as should the arguments, ideas and information they contain, without them being written in a grandstanding 'look at me' way.

Writer's economy

We've discovered elsewhere in this book that one of writing's truisms is that less is more. Sentences crammed with words, full stops, hyphens and brackets are usually harder to read than those that dispense with them and are kept simple. As with most writing rules, this isn't always true, as you are sometimes faced with linking complex or convoluted ideas and events together, and these require a certain amount of dexterity to marshal on the page.

> **'Producing a list allows you to stop juggling so many things in your head and concentrate on the words themselves.'**

Thinking about the order you want things to appear can help sometimes, so that you don't run into a mire of confusion, disjointed sequencing of information, and the subsequent frustration that you've left out some vital element, because you've been concentrating so hard on everything else.

If you're trying to stitch together a whole raft of connected things, sit down with a pen and paper and jot down the elements you have to write about in descending order of importance, starting with the one thing that justifies the story. Don't agonise too much about where all these elements should go. Once you've got something specific in front of you, it can be changed. Producing a list allows you to stop juggling so many things in your head and concentrate on the words themselves. Your list is the skeleton on which they can be hung. It requires a looser version of the news writer's mantra of 'who/what/why/when/where?', as you have some choice over which of these things is the most important part of the story.

You may ultimately decide that a part of the piece that did not initially strike you as its strongest or most interesting element is actually the thing that really makes it tick. If so, rewrite rather than ignore it. If it's a commission, and those who've asked you to produce it come to the same conclusion, they'll simply send it back to you and ask for changes.

Almost inevitably you'll have less time to make them, and anybody who says they haven't got time to sit and plan a story is deluding themselves. This isn't taking you away from the process of writing, it's part of that process, and unless you have an absolutely clear idea why you're writing something, you're in trouble.

> **'Unless you have an absolutely clear idea why you're writing something, you're in trouble.'**

Round in circles

One of the biggest giveaways that a writer is struggling with a story is when the same fact or facts are repeated over and over again. Working as a freelance editor for a print industry magazine, I had to tidy up a story about a new printing press. The story was about 1,000 words long, and started by referring to a feature that was unique to the machine. The writer returned to this feature four or five times during the course of his piece. He hadn't enough information, and rather than go back to the manufacturers to try and dig up some additional material, had simply rehashed his 'killer fact'.

I was forced to hack back the story, and was left with a slim item of about 400 words, and a 600-word gap to fill on the page. When challenged, the writer claimed there was nothing else to say – but was that true? There was nothing stopping him asking how easy the printer was to install, whether it would be cheaper to run, service, etc. He had stopped thinking or moved on to another job, and did not welcome being forced back to an item he believed was finished. I suspect that in due course the magazine stopped using him.

Fun on the page

Extraneous words ought to be purged, but where you have greater space to develop ideas and spread information in different paragraphs, take advantage of this and give the material space to breathe. You will also have more opportunity to play with language, finding interesting and original ways to use words, but don't try too hard here. It's very easy to become besotted with a way of describing a person, event or thing, only to discover that the way you've done this is over the top. Does a man with a prominent jaw line really have a face 'that juts like an Olympic diving board?' Does the crowd at a football match 'swarm like killer bees?' Is a new building's façade 'as enigmatic as the Mona Lisa's smile'? Hardly. These descriptions nearly work, but they're over-egging their subjects.

It's possible to have a jutting jaw line and football fans who 'swarm like bees'. As for the front of a building that resembles the enigmatic smile of a woman in a painting... Well, it doesn't, short of having Leonardo da Vinci's daub superimposed on it. You could perhaps write something about the enigmatic nature of the building's shape. However, as the Mona Lisa sentence proves, it's very easy to come up with a description that seems fine until you actually try decoding what it means, and find that it means nothing at all.

> 'It's very easy to become besotted with a way of describing a person, event or thing, only to discover that the way you've done this is over the top.'

Rhythm method

Write frequently and you'll start to notice that certain sentence structures have a rhythm to them that you find pleasing. They work so well that variations of them reappear in your work, sometimes deliberately, but often without you even realising. They're effective, offering a descriptive shortcut, or a neat way of expressing an idea or a feeling. Your brain will head for them automatically, especially if you're struggling to find a good way to start or finish a story.

David Gilmour, the Pink Floyd guitarist, described how musicians have a 'muscle memory', which leads them to familiar chord sequences, and said he had to work at not falling into this trap. The same applies to writing.

I reread a couple of stories I wrote for the same newspaper months after they appeared and experienced a nasty prickling sensation down my spine on realising that both ended in almost exactly the same way, with only two or three words separating their pay-offs.

Sometimes there's an element of necessary expediency. You know something will fit, so you use it, but the trick here is to keep thinking and keep trying to find original ways of using written language. This is ultimately more satisfying, and will always enhance your work.

Not doing so can also lead to unintended plagiarism, where you have read something by another writer which had such an impact that it stayed in your subconscious only to reappear in something you've written. Forgive yet another car-related recollection, but this happened to me. I read a barbed description of a car in which the writer 'lurched round corners and slouched uncomfortably in its marshmallow seats.' I knew just what he meant, and a decade on found I'd pinched the line word for word when describing an entirely different vehicle with similar deficiencies. I suspect nobody else noticed, but this description was part of a longer sentence, and yes, I'd accidentally pinched that too, and would have been in trouble if its creator had read my story. Imitation may be the sincerest form of flattery, but the imitated may not always see it that way.

Original thinking

If you've come across a good idea, and have managed to sell it to more than one outlet, a very good way to upset the people who've taken the story is to give them identical words. I've seen pieces in rival publications written by the same writer where entire sentences have been identical. If you're being paid twice, the least you can do is produce new words.

Be yourself

Even if you aren't a voracious reader, certain styles of writing and writers will almost certainly appeal to you. You might be thoroughly inspired by them, and this will almost certainly influence what you do with your own work. However, deliberately trying to copy other people's literary mannerisms and techniques is not to be recommended. Elements of what they do will probably filter into your writing anyway, and in the process of developing your own style it's both fun and instructive to play with different ideas and idioms to see which ones work for you. Again, by trying out turns of phrase, punctuation ideas and so forth, and binning those that don't fit, you'll gain the skills and knowledge that will allow you to access the ones that do.

> 'Deliberately trying to copy other people's literary mannerisms and techniques is not to be recommended.'

By contrast, words that are pale imitations of other people's will read awkwardly, because you've been concentrating on writing in a particular way instead of writing well.

Your views on what makes good writing might diverge strongly from mine. Many of the judgements we make about these things are subjective and personal, but people who write 'in the style of' are rarely as interesting to read as their inspirations. Instead, allow your own writing signature to emerge.

Stylish

A lot of publications have distinct 'house styles', showing how they expect people to write, but part of the enjoyment of journalistic writing is finding ways of meeting their criteria without feeling that you've completely betrayed the way you do things.

Double spacing the lines will leave room for insertions and corrections on handwritten or printed-out copies of work. And if you're one of the diminishing band who think typing is for typewriters and nothing else, then you can't be serious about writing for a living. Professionally, I would find it impossible to function as a writer if I couldn't type and didn't use a word processor.

Blocked

There often comes a point when getting going is tough, where the only answer is simply to get the information down on paper, or into a word processor, then look at it afterwards, editing and amending it at that point.

All you need

In the end, a good feature story should have a narrative spine to which the salient facts, figures and quotations are attached. Anybody reading it should not finish and wonder 'what was that all about?'

If you or your experiences are part of the story, there isn't an issue about these being included, or whether they're driving what's been written, but if they're not, and the story is about something to which you are an observer, your writing should be a conduit to get that information over to other

'A good feature story should have a narrative spine to which the salient facts, figures and quotations are attached.'

people. It really shouldn't overtly be about your opinions – unless you've been asked to give them, the item is a piece of first person commentary or an opinion piece, and this is what you've been expected to write.

Ultimately, a good feature story gives the reader something useful, thought provoking, interesting and perhaps surprising to read. If it has been commissioned, it should also meet the criteria set out by the person who asked for it, and your standards and aspirations. Sometimes these things are hard to marry up, but writers who get read, and get work, make sure that they do.

- **A dull introductory paragraph will turn off readers and editors alike. Make it fun, if appropriate, interesting and original – or all of these.**

- **If the subject interests you, don't assume others will share your enthusiasm.**

- **Apply critical detachment.**

- **Make your work accessible.**

- **Look for interest in the driest subject. You'll enjoy writing about it more and will find this easier.**

- **Be creative with your use of words, but don't over write, attempt to ape a style of writing, or a writer you admire.**

- **If in doubt about what to put in your story or leave out, draft a list.**

Chapter 5

CUT THE CRAP
How to self-edit

Are you keen to learn a foreign language? If so, perhaps
you would like to 'speak Italian like a Roman'?
Then again, perhaps not. I came across this gem in a
column of small ads. It was the work of a linguist keen to
pass on his skills, and I can only hope that his grasp of the
Italian language as it is spoken is better than his use of
English when written down.

Why? Simple. The Romans spoke Latin, not Italian. Yes I know the
natives of Rome the *city* speak Italian, and they might be
described as 'Romans', but Italian is the indigenous language of
modern Italy, and that innocent-looking, five-word phrase contains a
very clumsy mistake.

Such errors are all too easy to make. Sentences and paragraphs
that have more than one meaning, or are actually nonsense when read
over with a little more thought, are waiting in the shadows of your
brain, and will take great pleasure in leaping onto the page and
embarrassing you.

I once made the mistake of using the phrase 'sound and fury' when
describing a rally driver who was on the way to winning an event. This
was a lift from Shakespeare's *Macbeth*, and has become a piece of
descriptive writing shorthand. However, it had to go when a colleague
pointed out that the sentence from which it was lifted actually ran, 'It is
a tale told by an idiot, full of sound and fury, signifying nothing.' This

wasn't really the word picture I wanted to paint, and I suspect the rally man would have been less than amused if this clunker hadn't been spotted and put to death.

Not everyone would have noticed or cared, but given that you can't legislate for who will see what you've written, it's worth weeding out such anomalies before they get the chance. Taking the trouble to do so means that you've genuinely read what you've written, and where necessary changed it in a dispassionate way.

The incorrect use of words can also torture or tickle readers. Here's another small ad:

> Exploding organic health care business (people and animals) needs distributors.

Are the advertisers really looking for distributors to blow up people and animals with organic healthcare products, or is the business itself about to detonate?

I think what they're trying to say is that demand for their wares is 'exploding', but the word is in the wrong place and out of context, because it hasn't been explained. Really, something like: 'Successful human and animal healthcare products business seeks distributors' would have said the same thing without raising a titter.

Words can trip you up just by an unfortunate juxtaposition. So can the omission of words that 'bridge' subjects, people and happenings. I came across a classic example of this in a book manuscript, whose author, impatient to get her work under the noses of potential publishers, had sent it out without giving it a final, necessary polish. A single sentence described a small boy visiting his grandmother, and playing with his dog in her kitchen. It went something like this:

> Lewis's grandmother smiled as he played 'tug' with the spaniel. His ears flapped up and down wildly as they skidded across the kitchen floor.

Exactly whose ears are flapping up and down? Rationally we know they don't belong to the child, unless he has some horrible medical condition, and the writer is referring to the spaniel, but the sentence is badly constructed, and does not, in the strictest sense, make the distinction clear. It should. Detail of this sort ought to be explicit. Forcing the reader to second-guess what is meant really isn't good enough, nor is saying 'but isn't it obvious?' There ought to be no room for doubt or confusion, and left as it is, this sentence has a degree of accidental comedy to it.

Changing a few words would have made it entirely straightforward. So, it could have read:

> Lewis's grandmother smiled as he played 'tug' with the spaniel. The dog's ears flapped up and down wildly as he and Lewis skidded across the kitchen floor.

I've given ownership to the ears by using the words 'the dog's' Changing 'as they skidded across the kitchen floor' to 'as he and Lewis skidded' is being slightly pedantic, but I don't want any implication that it's the ears or grandmother who are doing the skidding.

Yes, I know the end product is a bit longer, that the title of this chapter is 'Cut the Crap', and one of the mantras of this book has been that simple is generally best, and simplicity and brevity often go together. However, if adding three or four words changes writing from grotty, woolly English into something that makes sense, then it's worth doing.

Does my sentence look long in this?

Another common pitfall is a wish to cram lots of information into sentences, making them overwritten, clumsy and punctuation-heavy. Anyone who has ground through a letter where each sentence and paragraph is weighed down with facts that meander on and on will groan at the memory.

More often than not these painfully top-heavy outpourings are the result of someone trying to think their way into a subject or a description, and read like the unspooling of mental processes that in reality they are.

You can see this in the repetition of ideas and words. Here's an example. 'The man came out of the dark alley. It was dark as the man appeared.' Either of these sentences would work perfectly well without the other.

On other occasions, these literary *faux pas* are the result of somebody attempting to be clever, to play with language or insert a phrase or sentence which appeals to them, and in the process simply trying too hard. If you want an example, how about this:

As a child I was born and raised within spitting distance (and I do mean spitting), of an ugly, glowering tower block whose windows – those that weren't broken that is!! – stared blankly from the concrete giant that loomed over its cowering inhabitants who scurried about along its concrete walkways, like an army of ants. Those walkways were like the tentacles of some great octopus when you looked down from the eighteenth floor, likely as not having had to climb the rubbish-strewn stairs first, because the lifts were more than likely to be broken, and watched old Mrs Wilson, or 'the cabbage baggage', as we called her in our little flat, walking towards the shops, or the bingo hall, or the social security office. This was the place I grew up. Not a place where you got a good start in life, and yet its very ugliness and despair made me determined to succeed and become the success I am today.

This is a single paragraph into which several paragraphs' worth of information have been squeezed, and it's made of sentences where information spills from one to the next, rather than being contained singly in each.

It starts with a pair of admittedly mild clichés ('I was born and raised within spitting distance…'), words are repeated too closely to each other ('the concrete giant that loomed over its cowering inhabitants who scurried about along its concrete walkways' – too much concrete), and readers are confronted by a forest of commas over which they can trip, in the process disturbing the flow and ease of reading. Ditto the intrusive brackets, dashes and – horror of horrors – those two exclamation marks. They are the equivalent of grabbing the reader by the collar and screaming into his ear, over-emphasising a point that's being made in passing. The end result looks amateurish. Do you GET MY DRIFT??!!!

Forests of exclamation marks belong in frothing letters exchanged between retired colonels about the dreadful state of the modern world, and not in anything that aspires to be written to a professional standard. Put simply, exclamation marks should be used singly, and sparingly, or they lose their impact.

Having got this particular rant out of the way, let's get back to the never-ending paragraph. The writer has obviously become carried away in his enthusiasm to create a picture of what's being described. It's the classic 'chuck in everything including the kitchen sink' approach. What remains is overwritten (did everybody who walked past this building 'cower'? I rather doubt it), and some of the phrases need to go or be spaced out so the ones that remain have room to stand out.

'Exclamation marks should be used singly, and sparingly, or they lose their impact.'

Let's try and untangle things a little with some rewriting:

My childhood was spent in the shadow of an ugly tower block. Its blank, often broken windows stared down on the people who scurried like ants along its concrete walkways. Climbing the stairs to the eighteenth floor (the lift was often broken), and looking down on our neighbours far below, those paths seemed like concrete tentacles.

We watched people like old Mrs Wilson walking towards the shops, social security office or bingo hall. We called her 'the cabbage baggage', and like that tower block she was part of the often ugly and despairing world I grew up in. Escaping from this world was to be my spur to succeed later in life.

Now about 100 words long, the same information is contained in two short paragraphs rather than a single long one running to 160 words. We've junked some of the awkward attempts at wordplay (removing the clichéd 'spitting distance' is a prime example), and changed the end so that it no longer reads in quite such a self-congratulatory tone, and sits more easily with the rest of the sentences.

And another thing

It's equally easy to turn shorter sentences into literary dirges. You've probably read something along the lines of:

It was on Saturday, January 24th, with an overcast sky, on a typical grey, weekend shopping day, when I prepared to head for the shops, slammed the front door of my terraced house and reaching into my raincoat pocket found that I'd left my wallet on the hall table, and the house keys, so I couldn't get back in again!

This sort of thing makes you want to scream 'get on with it!' Remember too that this gem is 60 words long. It chumbles and bumbles flaccidly towards a conclusion that is painfully obvious after about the first 20 words. The answer then, is to take a scalpel to it, like this:

It was a grey January Saturday when I slammed the front door and realised my keys and wallet were still in the house. The shopping trip would have to wait.

This takes 30 words to say the same thing. Now let's return to the other horrors tied up in its flabby predecessor.

> It was on Saturday, January 24th [why do we need to know the exact date?], with an overcast sky, on a typical grey, weekend shopping day [who cares if it's 'typical' and why is there a second reference to the weather?], when I prepared to head for the shops [yes, yes, how fascinating], slammed the front door of my terraced house [as opposed to your flat, penthouse, shed, etc. – if the exact nature of your domicile becomes important to the narrative, mention it later], and reaching into my raincoat pocket [more detail which should be slipped in further into the story], found that I'd left my wallet on the hall table, and the house keys, so I couldn't get back in again! [Why not simply write, 'then found I'd left my wallet and house keys on the hall table'? You lose a word and two commas, tie together the pair of connected items – wallet and keys – and don't have the order of information broken up with references to the table in the middle of the sentence. The last-gasp information about being locked out is made even more laboured by the exclamation mark. It's unnecessarily ramming home a pretty obvious point.]

Again, three to four paragraphs' worth of information has been brutally hammered into a single sentence. This is the writing equivalent of trying to squeeze a week's worth of clothes into an overnight bag.

Pace yourself

Good writing has a rhythm and pace to it that readers will pick up and which, with practice, you can learn to recognise. Sentences also have a sense of pace. The way some are written means they are read at a canter, others rush by, and it's possible to break up a sentence using full stops and commas so that it has an almost staccato feel, and brings the reader up short. For example:

> The wrecking ball swung and connected with the wall. Cracks appeared, as brickwork absorbed the impact with a muffled thud. A brief lull. Then like a fist punching something six feet beyond its intended target, the ball struck again. Bang! The wall imploded as the ball drove through it. Bricks fanned out followed by billowing dust. Then the wrecking ball emerged, jumping and shuddering on its chain.

There's nothing languid about this description, thanks to the full stops, and only three commas are used. However, it's equally possible to present the same information in an entirely different way, just by changing the odd word and altering the punctuation, like this:

> When the wrecking ball swung into the wall, cracks appeared in the brickwork, as it absorbed the impact with a muffled thud. This was followed by a brief lull as the ball was winched back. Then it struck again, like a fist punching something six feet beyond its intended target, and drove through the wall with a loud bang. The impact caused bricks and dust to fan out, and through this the now shuddering, jumping wrecking ball soon emerged.

Not again

It's important to weed out repeated words. If you don't, your work will be leaden to read. For instance, you could write:

> 'The dog always hates going to the vet. Once we get to the vet the dog almost has to be dragged out of the car, and when we get to the waiting room he lies on the floor and shivers.'

This is an obvious construct, and you'd have to work hard to get quite so many repetitions into a single sentence, but such things do creep into most people's work, especially if they are in 'get it down now, look at it later' mode. However, the whole thing can easily be rescued from repetition misery. Here's an example:

> The dog always hates going to the vet, and almost has to be dragged out of the car when we arrive. Once inside the waiting room, he lies on the floor and shivers.

Read it

Spotting errors and lumpen sentences means closely examining what you've written. Reading what's on the page, not what your brain fondly imagines is there, is the best way to achieve this, whether the words have come easily, or had to be dragged reluctantly into the world like screaming babies.

If you've written something with a word processor, print off a copy, perhaps changing the font or font size, so what you see on paper looks different from the on-screen version. Make it double spaced to allow notes and corrections to be added.

'Reading the words out loud is a good way to take your brain off autopilot, because you can't skim over them.'

If I'm really concentrating, I'll put a sheet of paper directly under the line of text I'm reading and shift this downwards as I go. This technique forces a reader to really examine the words, punctuation and grammar.

Reading the words out loud is another good way to take your brain off autopilot, because you can't skim over them. You've got to concentrate on every aspect of the work, down to the last full stop and comma. If they break up sentences in the wrong way, present information badly or repeat it, you will hear this.

Some well established writers use these methods, and some get friends or colleagues to read their work. Don't be afraid to do the same. A second pair of eyes will often see things that you haven't.

Nothing's sacred

If something has proved tricky to write, is a cherished idea for a sentence, or something that you're particularly pleased with, the temptation not to change it is often strong, but that temptation should be resisted. It's very easy to be blinded to the faults of the ones you love. After all, those words are your babies.

In isolation, a paragraph can seem expressive and polished. However, it may not sit comfortably with the words around it, and jar with them as a result. Equally, it might not have the articulacy and flow that you imagined it possessed, or simply be rather contrived.

There's an old writing adage that the sentence you think is the best thing you've ever written is the one that should go because you can't look at it objectively, and it's strange how often this proves to be true. So the next time you come up with a small gem, cut it and replace it with some expediently written words. You'll be surprised how little the rest of the piece loses by its absence, or how much it gains in cohesiveness.

- Simple sentences are best.

- Read aloud what you've written, or get others to read it. This will expose punctuation, grammar or factual problems.

- Don't cram too much information into each sentence and paragraph. Start a new sentence when you have a new fact or detail.

- Playing with words that create images on the page is good, but don't do this constantly. Bombarding your readers with literary pyrotechnics will tire them out.

- Nothing is sacred. Be prepared to edit out any element of an item you've written, if it makes the end product better.

Chapter 6

THE CURSE OF THE CLICHÉ
How to escape from hackneyed hell

I should be on to a win-win situation with this chapter.
I can bite the bullet and really make it punch above its
weight, vis-à-vis the other chapters in this book.
Oh dear, the cliché. It crops up in people's spoken and
written language, and it's awful.

Clichés are used to disguise a lack of knowledge, dress up something ordinary and banal as special or unique, add credibility to the fatuous, and when verbalised seem engineered to fill a vacuum with another vacuum. They are also often at the apex of insincerity. When a man in a suit says, 'I hear what you're saying', you know for certain that he is not listening.

When I become dictator, the person who decided that the word 'solutions' had a life beyond being the plural of 'solution' (viz. 'Anthrax: for death procurement solutions'), will be hunted down by a slavering pack of dogs and killed.

My *Chambers Concise Dictionary* describes the word cliché as 'a stereotyped phrase, or literary tag: something hackneyed as idea, plot, situation'. Mind you, it also suggests that the word relates to 'an electrotype or stereotype plate', and no, I couldn't tell you what those things do, although if either of them is big and heavy, dropping one on a literary cliché-monger might be a very good idea. Please excuse the rant, but when you see these things over and over again, for years on end, they become ever more hateful.

A single word can assume the mantle of cliché. If you want to be absolutely accurate, such words should also be described as 'hackneyed'. Something which is hackneyed is used too often, so it becomes commonplace and boring. I don't see why this should exclude it from being filed under 'cliché', along with all those terrible phrases beloved of estate agents, politicians, local councillors and management consultants.

A good example is 'delicious'. It is a useful, descriptive word, and yet there's something about its very ubiquity – 'delicious' gets everywhere – that in certain circumstances makes it clichéd. 'Thank you for the delicious meal' is an entirely innocent phrase, but it's deeply obvious. How many times have you read that particular set of words? They're tired and unoriginal, and it's this lack of originality that tips 'delicious' into the cliché category. In other contexts (e.g. a sentence that reads 'a delicious mix of innocence and cynicism') the word is entirely blameless. Replacing 'delicious' in our 'thank you for feeding us' missive – and there are plenty of alternative words that fit the bill; even 'lovely' would do – neuters its cliché credentials.

You might be reading this and shaking your head. Perhaps you think that the word is merely being used in context, and as such does not offend you – but there is an element of subjectivity in our likes and dislikes about writing. For me 'delicious' comes near the top of the list of words to avoid.

Another word that has plenty of cliché potential is 'leading'. I know several journalists who use it almost constantly when describing businesses and people. So, they're never writing about garages or plumbers' merchants. Instead, they're 'leading providers of vehicle maintenance solutions' (yes, it's the 's-word' again), or 'leading sanitation supply specialists'.

No, no, no! They fix cars and sell ballcocks. In both contexts the word 'leading' is redundant, because in reality they aren't leading anybody in a physical sense. (Incidentally, are their rivals 'trailing' providers?)

OK, we do know why the word has been used in this way. The idea is to demonstrate that the companies it is describing are better than their rivals, or are at the top of the sector in which they do business, but to call them 'successful' would say the same thing. If they're genuinely at the top of the car-fixing and lavatory parts worlds, then this should be obvious in what's written about them, and you could then ditch the word 'leading'.

Anyhow, describing them as 'leading' instantly gives the sentence concerned the clunking predictability of a piece of second-rate advertising copy.

Another hardy perennial singular cliché is 'funky', a word used by the middle-aged to describe things that they fondly believe the young find trendy and fashionable. Car makers love 'funky', and will resort to it when describing the dullest small hatchback. Everything from interior trim patterns to plastic bumpers are 'funky', and I'll wager that very few mobile phone designs have not had this word applied to them at one time or another. There are equally horrible derivations, of which 'funkster' deserves special mention. This is not a disco-dancing hamster, but is likely to be applied to somebody who works in the music or fashion industries. Here is a word conjured up by a journalist desperate for a hip, happening piece of writing shorthand to describe an individual.

However you mangle it, 'funky' is a cliché because it is overused and actually doesn't mean a whole lot. What it once meant is less than lovely, according to the jazz singer and humorist George Melly. He said the word 'funk' originated in the American Deep South, and was used to describe the smell given off by less than hygienic people. Having discovered this, I hope you will view the word in a wholly new light, and resist the temptation to use it.

In the world of cliché, hills are always 'rolling', roads 'winding', a person who is pleased looks like 'the cat who's got the cream', while leaving it too late to put something right is 'shutting the stable door after the horse has bolted', and so on, and on, ad infinitum.

Such phrases and words have a common usage, and a usefulness, because they convey ideas with a certain economy, but using them over and over again knocks out the originality in a person's writing, and makes it tired, formulaic and sometimes nonsensical, viz.

> The actor's weekend cottage nestles at the feet of rolling hills, and is reached by a winding country road. When he greets us, still fresh from his latest movie triumph, he looks like the cat that's got the cream. Hardly surprising, as his latest role has undoubtedly made him the cream of the crop in Hollywood. Directors who previously shunned him have been bombarding his agent with enquiries about working for them.

This is pedestrian and also mixes its metaphors ('the cat that's got the cream' and 'cream of the crop'). Let's try and get across the same information in a different way:

> You really need a compass and a map reference to find the actor's cottage. Hidden at the end of a twisting country lane and dwarfed by the surrounding hills, it's not an obvious venue for meeting a man whose once-moribund Hollywood movie career is enjoying a dramatic revival. With directors who once shunned him now clamouring for his services, it's a place he's had little time to enjoy recently.

I'm not claiming that this is a fabulously constructed, fantastically original piece of writing, but it does avoid recycling other people's done-to-death words. (As an aside, I've never really known which crop produces cream – surely you need cows?) It does try to give readers a sense of place, create an image in their minds, and still lets them know that a thespian bloke whose career was in trouble is once more busy and successful, while editing out some extraneous stuff about his agent.

And another thing!

There are plenty of other cliché candidates. How about 'cool'? A word with a specific meaning about not being warm, a state of mind or a persona. It can also be applied to something trendy, but it's been done to death, and once again, the dregs of the advertising copywriting industry have spent decades mating it to funky and indeed 'hot', when describing the latest consumer durables. There are manufacturers of electric toasters who describe their products as 'funky and cool', when perhaps 'hot sometimes' would be a lot more accurate.

Should you have a disaster involving your toaster exploding and your fridge melting, this dual misfortune will be described as a 'double whammy'. However, if your life be blighted solely by one of these appliances packing up, you wouldn't call the problem a 'whammy'. I bet if you asked people who used the term exactly what a 'whammy' is, they'd struggle to say.

The world of business, home of the aforementioned 'win-win situation', is groaning under the weight of clichéd writing, and it's hard to know where to start when thinking of the quasi-scientific, pseudo evangelical guff that is spewed out in the name of commerce.

How about 'customer facing activities'? As far as I know this means 'talking to customers', but apparently that sounds too ordinary (see also 'customer focus'). Company departments don't fit together; they have 'synergies'. We no longer buy things, instead we invest in 'customer propositions'. Should we have a preference for a particular maker or supplier of these goods, we are apparently investing in 'brand values', because the owners of these famous names have 'core values' that consumers like or aspire to.

As a fully paid-up member of the grumpy middle-aged tendency, I still labour under the impression that a brand is something applied to a cow's backside as proof of ownership, and a core belongs inside an apple. Of course the meanings of words and phrases change – and this goes beyond mere dictionary definitions – but the repetitive, careless or crass use of these words has given them cliché status. They have become literary stodge, used to bulk up weak and poor writing, or fill large gaps in a writer's imagination.

Rhyme without reason

Push certain words together and the way they sound becomes clichéd. This is often done as part of a process known as alliteration, and is generally where similar sounds or even rhythms recur. There's nothing wrong with this as such. It's part of most people's speech patterns and writing, and can be clever, funny and charming, but naff alliterative phrases should irritate the hell out of all right-thinking persons. Anyway, leading contenders include 'temptingly tasty'. What could be worse than this? Well, 'temptingly tasty toffee' for a start. Yes, gentle reader, 'temptingly tasty' has it all, being corny, meaningless rubbish. Also, you would need to possess a literary tin ear not to be offended by the twee rhythm made if you say it aloud – I dare you to try this and not feel a shudder of disgust. Nothing is ever 'temptingly tasty'. It is 'good', 'great', 'special', 'delicious' (only joking), even 'nice' (a rather wimpish word, but descriptive enough).

> **'Naff alliterative phrases should irritate the hell out of all right-thinking persons.'**

Home-made

It's entirely possible to make your own clichés, by knotting together words and phrases that don't add up to anything when examined for meaning. One of the most miserable professional experiences of my life was working for a magazine where my immediate boss could barely string a coherent sentence together, and edited other people's copy with the care and sensitivity of someone drowning a bag of kittens in a river.

Here was a man who could write: 'Mr Parkinson's coup has undoubtedly been his windfall.' Come again? This, surely, has all the hallmarks of cliché. He's managed to use 'coup' and 'windfall' in the same sentence, without them having any real context, and it's not obvious what it is he's attempting to say. Finding personal and original ways of expressing yourself on the page is always more interesting than dredging up a lot of hoary old literary standbys.

'Finding personal and original ways of expressing yourself on the page is always more interesting than dredging up a lot of hoary old literary standbys.'

You will find the good stuff by not trying too hard, and have a lot more entertainment playing around with words and word pictures. These will work most effectively when they're not contrived. Take a look at what you have to write about and just describe what you see or hear. If something needs explaining, ask yourself, 'how does that make sense to me?' and use this as your writing template.

For some of us, there's a confidence gap, which we tend to fill with clichés and, of course, there are words, sayings and phrases that have become clichés simply because they are true, or their meanings are widely understood. Often, this is why they're so popular, but in the end, your writing will be more distinctive and better for their absence.

Even if you do not believe you have an original turn of phrase, or a passion for the written word, you do have a distinct 'authorial voice', and with decent use of spelling, grammar and punctuation, this will be perfectly serviceable on the page. And remember, writing as yourself is always preferable, as the words you produce will have a mix of authenticity, authority and even originality that will set them apart from much of the derivative, literary slurry that gets churned out every day.

- **Resorting to cliché shows a lack of interest or thought.**

- **Finding an original way of expressing things rather than relying on cliché will improve your writing.**

- **Politicians use clichés. This does not recommend them.**

- **Yesterday's clever turn of phrase can be today's cliché.**

Chapter 7

AN EXPLANATION OF PUNCTUATION
Every dot and comma

This chapter won't tell you everything about the
knotty problems associated with punctuation. To do that
you'll need to read one of the many books
completely devoted to the subject, but it should
be useful as an aide-mémoire.

Given the language's abbreviated nature, I've concentrated on English, rather than American English punctuation forms, and stuck to the basics. Writing this chapter made clear some things I knew instinctively, but couldn't remember being taught, showed up areas of sloppiness in the way I punctuate, a few things I didn't know and one or two bad habits I needed to correct. Which ones? Well, they're for me to know and you, hopefully, not to find out.

The apostrophe

Let's start with the apostrophe (') which gives people a lot of grief. It tells you when a word is possessive (something belongs to its subject) or a contraction (when a longer word has been abbreviated or shortened), but has some other less obvious applications. Perversely, in a few cases where you would expect it to appear it doesn't, but sadly, incorrect use of this irritating little item will make your writing look amateurish and illiterate.

Possessed

Using the apostrophe to give words a possessive meaning is where we often come unstuck. 'Sandev's car' is a possessive, because the car belongs to him. Likewise, 'Jane's computer'. Read either as 'Sandevs car' or 'Janes computer' and they suddenly look rather peculiar. You may have seen shop sign writing where this error has been made (e.g. 'Terrys Flower Shop') and winced on behalf of the owner.

The possessive apostrophe can also be applied to inanimate things, such as 'the computer's keyboard' or 'the lawnmower's blade'. Not being alive doesn't exclude them from possessing other items.

Generally, an apostrophe is inserted between the word being given a possessive tag and the letter 's', as in 'the building's revolving doors', because if you are writing about one building, the word in singular form does not end with an 's'. However, other words in plural noun form often do. We'll come to nouns later, but here are some examples of them where you need apostrophes to denote ownership:

The schools' playgrounds
The ladies' club
The neighbours' houses

When used possessively, each gains an apostrophe at its end, but not an additional letter 's'. Why? Well, just try saying 'schools's', 'ladies's' or 'neighbours's' without tying your tongue in a knot. Using the way these words are spoken in this context is a reliable guide to how they should be written, likewise people's names naturally ending with 's' ('James' for instance).

The other exceptions are pronouns (see page 98), often, although not exclusively, written in the present tense. Such as:

Which deckchairs are ours?
Where are my house keys?
The house lost its roof in the storm.

In the first two cases, the words 'my' and 'our' are the possessive forms of the pronouns 'me' and 'us'. The word itself ('my' or 'our') tells you that possession is involved and so does the job of an apostrophe and 's'. Therefore, the sentences 'Which deckchairs are ours?' and 'Where are my house keys?' are correct as they are, without any possessive apostrophe being introduced. If you tried to add an apostrophe, you'd need to write 'Which deckchairs are us's?' or 'Where are me's house keys?', which sounds wrong enough to warn you that you don't need to.

With 'the house lost its roof in the storm', you can't insert an apostrophe into the word 'its' so it becomes 'it's', because in that case the word's meaning is changed to 'it is', rendering the sentence meaningless. This is because the apostrophe is also used to combine and shorten words, as we'll discover a few paragraphs from now.

Another horror in this area is the confusion between 'whose' and 'who's'. The former is a possessive word ('whose shoes are those?'). The latter is the result of combining 'who' and 'is', so instead of writing 'who is that girl?', you abbreviate it to 'who's that girl?'

Modern punctuation has been arrived at by a process of evolution, changes in taste and refinement of language rather than logic – which might dictate that we dispense with apostrophes completely – so in cases like the car keys sentence, it's a matter of looking at the meaning of what has been written and working out whether an apostrophe is appropriate or not.

Shrink!

Using apostrophes for stitching words together is known as writing 'contractions', and has nothing to do with the advanced stages of pregnancy. Instead it refers to a pair of words being combined, with one *generally* cut down, the apostrophe marking where a letter has been left out. Most such words are verbs, and we use them a great deal, for example: 'it's ('it is'), 'they've' ('they have'), 'he'll' ('he will'), 'aren't' ('are not') and so on. (As an aside, this is also the case when it comes to dates: for example, the 1960s and the 1970s become the '60s and the '70s – as opposed to the 60's and 70's – the apostrophe again showing where something has been left out.)

An already contracted word can be given this treatment for a second time. An extreme example of this is 'We'd've', which is a melding together of 'we would have'. This is not actually good written English, and once I'd written it my word processor flagged it up as a misspelling. However, it could be used as an example of colloquial, or spoken English, if used in a quotation ('"We'd've found our way home with a decent map," said Mark Thatcher').

Regular contractions are useful when you need to get things over in a limited number of words, or if the meaning of a sentence otherwise requires a repetition of certain words. An example of this would be: 'She'll soon pack her suitcase for the last time, and says she will miss her friends.'

Written as 'She will soon pack her suitcase for the last time, and says she will miss her friends', it becomes a little bit clumsy, thanks to the reappearance of 'she' and 'will' in the same sentence. Again, we see how something that would be quite acceptable if spoken, is less so when written. As with other punctuation marks, overusing apostrophes also looks awkward on the page, so they shouldn't be applied indiscriminately. Finding different ways of getting ideas over is always preferable.

Rules and exceptions

Unless possession is involved, apostrophes aren't applied to plural words or names (those which denote more than one thing or person) where an 's' has been added. Examples include 'telephones', 'horses', and phrases like, 'the Osmonds are still touring'. A classic example of breaking this rule would be a market trader's sign that read, 'tomato's for sale'.

Sentences where there are possessive elements and therefore apostrophes include 'the goats' beards' or 'the horses' paddock'. The main rule for applying apostrophes is that they donate omissions or possessions, but generally should not be applied to plurals.

There are inevitably some exceptions. Apostrophes are required for letters of the alphabet (a's, c's, etc.), and phrases such as 'do's and don'ts'. Here, the apostrophe separates an 's' from the main word to which it is attached, so there is no confusion about the resultant word's meaning (what's a 'dos' when it's at home?). Often there is no potential for confusion, so an apostrophe applied to the words concerned would be redundant (think 'telephone' and 'telephones', 'door' and 'doors', etc.)

The full stop

Compared to some punctuation marks, the full stop is blissfully straightforward to use. It ends a sentence containing a statement or specific piece of information, such as:

The camera was big.
The dog scratched its ear.
My trousers are frayed at the edges.

You'll find full stops within paragraphs containing more than one statement. So:

The camera was big. It sat on a wooden tripod.
The dog scratched its ear. It had fleas again.
My trousers are frayed at the edges. I need a new pair.

In every case here, substituting the first full stop for a comma would be wrong (viz. 'The dog scratched its ear, it had fleas again.') because that comma implies that each part of the sentence is about the same statement or fact. Full stops make it clear that they each have one subject. In many cases you can insert a joining or connecting word ('and', 'so', 'but', 'because', etc.), although this can alter a sentence's meaning. Here are some examples:

The camera was big and it sat on a wooden tripod.
The dog scratched its ear because it had fleas again.
My trousers are frayed at the edges, so I need a new pair.

Questions

Of course, the rules of English are fluid, and many sentences aren't concluded with a full stop. Instead they finish with a question mark (?) or an exclamation mark (!). You will never see something along the lines of 'are you sure?.'

Question marks are applied to sentences where a question is asked directly, such as: 'Are you ready to go out?' or 'Why is the plumber repairing the oven?' However, when questions are asked indirectly, the question mark isn't used ('he asked why the plumber was repairing the oven' and 'they asked how many goldfish were in my pond').

When something is uncertain, question marks can find themselves between a pair of brackets. An example of this would be: 'The poem is thought to have been inspired by a nun called "Martha the Mysterious" (?)'. That bracketed question mark indicates that Martha's true name is itself a bit of a mystery.

Exclamation marks. Really? Yes!

This is a useful item to finish a sentence where something is being strongly expressed. Here are some candidates:

What an ugly baby!
Look at that!
Hello, big boy!

Exclamation marks crop up in written examples of speech, when ideas, emotions, etc., are vigorously described, e.g.:

I spent five years building that!
She cried, 'nobody understands!'
Finally, I'm free!

Such things can be applied to journalism, but generally, exclamation marks should be used sparingly whatever you're writing, or your work will start to look rather hysterical.

This means that you should avoid using exclamation marks unnecessarily (as in, 'avoid using exclamation marks unnecessarily!'), and unless you're writing a private letter, never use more than one, as people will think you are bonkers!!!

See what I mean?

The complex comma

Commas (,) are innocuous looking punctuation squiggles with many and varied applications. They break up sentences, giving the reader a mental pause for breath (instead of 'They break up sentences giving the reader a mental pause for breath,' which has probably left you rather winded). They can be used as a substitute for words used to link information, making them useful mediums for splitting that information into readable chunks where full stops wouldn't be appropriate.

Commas can also be applied to sentences where information is all-of-a-piece, but requires a soft form of punctuation, such as: 'Once hatched, and having pumped up its wings, the dragonfly only lives for a few days.'

When commas are used in this way, you should be able to chop out the information they surround and still be left with a sentence that makes sense. In this case: 'Once hatched, the dragonfly only lives for a few days.'

If this isn't so, you've gone wrong grammatically. Here's an example: 'No, he wouldn't wear nylon socks, as they make his feet itch.' Strike out 'he wouldn't wear nylon socks', and you're left with: 'No, as they make his feet itch', which doesn't make a lot of sense in isolation.

In this context, commas make a good substitute for the words 'and' and 'or', in sentences that list things, for instance: 'Birds, cats, dogs and sheep aren't natural bedfellows.' Without commas you'd be forced to write something like: 'Birds and cats and dogs and sheep aren't natural bedfellows,' resulting in a sentence that reads like a slightly perverse Eurovision Song Contest lyric.

> **'Commas make a good substitute for the words "and" and "or", in sentences that list things.'**

Let's try something similar where commas have allowed the word 'or' to be given a rest. Here goes: 'I couldn't decide between vanilla, raspberry or chocolate ice cream.' Better than 'vanilla or raspberry or chocolate', don't you think?

Using commas in this way allows for a string of linked information to be joined together in single sentences, but neither completely dispenses with 'and' or 'or'. These remain when describing the final items of each, so that the sentences don't fall to pieces grammatically ('I couldn't decide between vanilla, raspberry, chocolate ice cream' reads like a piece of hurried note taking).

Sentences that do not, in the strict sense, list their contents, can also be joined together by commas, as long as an appropriate connecting word is also used. Here are a few examples.

- The jetty was easy to see, but surrounding rocks made reaching it a tricky business.
- The man waited nervously by the wall, as the knife thrower prepared to use him in his act.
- I wanted to eat another cream bun, yet I knew it would make me sick.

It's very easy to drop commas into text inappropriately, so that if you isolate what has been highlighted by them, it doesn't make sense. 'The flowers are wildly, swaying caught in the Westerly breeze' is an example. Can flowers ever be 'wildly'? Not really, nor can anything be 'swaying caught'. However, they can be 'wildly swaying', and shifting the comma so that the sentence now reads 'The flowers are wildly swaying, caught in the Westerly breeze', results in everything making perfect sense.

You might think that such a punctuation oddity sticks out like a sore thumb, and you'd be right, but it's amazing how a writer's mind can play tricks, so that glaringly obvious errors like this are missed.

As an aside, it might be possible to re-jig the sentence's order of information and get rid of that comma, so you'd end up with something like 'The Westerly breeze made the flowers sway wildly'. This little piece of re-writing means fewer words, less room for confusion, and ultimately, less hassle.

Commas also make useful substitutions for words that would otherwise need repeating, and allow related things to be joined together. 'One telephone is in the hall, the other in the lounge,' is an example (instead of 'One telephone is in the hall. The other telephone is in the lounge').

Space precludes going into detail about all the ways commas are used, but the main thing to remember is that applied properly, they make your words easier to read, assisting in the way they flow on the page. Scattered about indiscriminately, they will turn your writing into a stuttering mess.

Colons

Why does the word 'colon' have both medical and literary meanings? I realise this is a slightly childish question, which might not be asked if the word with the double meaning was *rib*, but *colon*'s schizophrenic nature is very much a feature of the English language.

The colon used in punctuation (:) has one major function. It implies that the information which follows it amplifies and explains the clause or phrase preceding it, for instance:

It was pitch black: he couldn't find the light switch.
She listed her rivals: David, Hannah and John.
Another mile to go: they wouldn't give up now.

Note that words following colons don't start with a capital letter (unless they're names), except when you're writing in American English.

Semi-detached

The semicolon (;) works as a halfway house between the comma and full stop, where the subject matter of a sentence is not obviously self contained – so automatically requiring a full stop – but nor is it so closely linked that a comma works adequately as a means of splitting it up.

The semicolon can also be used to tighten up sentences where dividing words such as 'but' or 'and' do not sit comfortably on the page.

However, each part of a sentence where a semicolon is used should still make complete

'Each part of a sentence where a semicolon is used should still make complete sense if split from the other.'

sense if split from the other, so it would be incorrect to use a semicolon to write, 'He climbed into bed and winced; the hot water bottle had leaked,' because although both elements of this sentence aren't nonsense when read in isolation, they lose their context and specific meaning when read separately. However, the semicolon slots in perfectly with, 'The original Star Wars movie appeared in 1977; the final Star Wars film, 'Revenge of the Sith', debuted in 2004.'

Choices

An element of personal judgement will sometimes be required when using these punctuation marks, because they stress different things in what you are writing, and can switch the meanings of otherwise identical sentences. This can be enjoyable and useful if you know what you're doing, but will throw your readers off course if you do not.

So, 'Jack was lost. His belongings hadn't reached the airport,' tells you two separate facts thanks to the full stop. Jack hasn't a clue where he is, and his belongings have been mislaid, but write this as, 'Jack was lost: his belongings hadn't reached the airport,' and the sentence implies that Jack is lost *because* his belongings have gone missing. These are both bad scenarios for Jack, but their meanings and implications are distinct.

Big ideas. Capital letters.

Do you need to know that sentences always start with capital letters? Probably not, but since their other uses flow from this, it ought to be mentioned. Dates, days, months and years are always capitalised, likewise languages ('German', 'Urdu', etc.). Seasons are not, unless the time of year being written about starts a sentence, so 'Autumn is the time to dig up your potatoes' is fine, but 'Your potatoes should be dug up in the Autumn' is not.

Words that denote nationalities, races, etc. ('Caucasian', 'Lebanese') always start with a capital letter, as do names and professional titles ('Doctor', 'Professor', 'Engineer') when applied to specific individuals. So writing about 'Professor Jane Turner' would be fine, but a line of text that reads 'the bioengineering laboratory was suddenly filled with white-coated Professors' is wrong, because it's describing professors generically rather than an individual.

If you were writing about the 'courage of Dutch resistance fighters in World War Two', the word 'Dutch' would be capitalised because it refers to a specific nationality. The more general 'He needed dutch courage to ask her out' is legitimate, because the term 'dutch courage' is descriptive rather than specific, but just to confuse things, you could also write it as 'Dutch courage' and be correct. If you're more comfortable with this form, make sure it's used consistently.

Specific names of places, bodies and items should be started with capital letters. This means the 'Louvre Museum in Paris' gets a capital letter 'M', but for 'Parisian art museums', stick with a lower case 'm'. Likewise, use capital first letters in 'The World Bank's debt repayment policies', but not in 'the world's bankers'. The same rule applies when 'buying an Aga Cooker', rather than 'buying a cooker'. You would not buy 'a Cooker', as this would imply some odd, street-slang job title for a chef ('cheeky Cooker Jamie Oliver' perhaps? Then again, perhaps not).

Historical periods ('The Dark Ages') get initial capital letters, and so do many religious names and customs. 'God' always gets a capital 'g', but the word can be written in lower case when used in a non-specific way ('The gods were smiling on him,' etc.).

If you're writing about something with a title, such as a play or a book, generally that title's important words should be capitalised only if this is in UK English; so *The Lord of the Rings* rather than *The Lord Of The Rings*, and *The Taming of the Shrew* instead of *The Taming Of The Shrew* are good examples.

Going large

Occasionally the capitalisation of a series of words can be used to give emphasis to a sentence, for example:

> My boss was furious. With jowls quivering, he told me that blowing things up in the car park 'WOULD NOT BE TOLERATED'.

This does however rather shove them under a reader's nose, and it is something that should be used sparingly. Putting the words you would like to emphasise into italics is a more subtle way of achieving a similar kind of result.

Capitals can be used to good effect when adding irony to a sentence ('the drunken holiday makers didn't expect to get arrested. After all, they were the Beautiful People'). Written this way the words 'beautiful people' take on a sarcastic feel.

Italics

Used to give words or phrases emphasis, italics are a useful way of conveying a feeling, contrasting something or drawing a reader's attention. Here are some examples.

- 'He knew the will would make him rich if only he could find it. How he wished he could *see*,' which emphasises the person's frustration.
- 'The dog's habit of digging up the flower bed gave him *huge* pleasure' (the italicised word denotes feeling – the dog is having a great time).
- 'We were told the road would be repaired within days. In fact it took *six weeks*,' illustrates the contrast between what was promised, and what was actually delivered.
- 'The *smallness* of the bricks used showed that the manor house dated back to the 16th century,' points the reader towards a particular feature of the building being described.

Often technical phrases, biological, specialist, medical and even plant names are italicised when given in full, likewise when quoting works of reference. In this instance, italics are used to draw the reader's attention to the fact that the source information quoted has come from other people's work.

Please excuse my going on, but once again you don't want to resort to italics too frequently. As with many things in punctuation, the more they're used, the less impact they have.

Quotation marks

When using quotation or speech marks for direct quotations, the decision on whether they will be in single (') or double (") form will depend very much on which part of the world you live, or for whom you are writing. Publications have different house styles, and will favour one or the other.

However, when a direct quotation is topped and tailed by them in either form, their use is clear. You are reading something that a person has said. So, '"My daughter has feet the size of sideboards," said Mrs Skinner' contains a direct quotation. '"I have done nothing that warrants my resignation," said Pensions Minister, Philip Gordon', is another. The double quotation marks indicate that this is a contained quote within another, and tell you that the main quote is not finished until you reach the single quotation mark.

Translating spoken English to the page sometimes renders what has been said as meaningless unless it has been amplified or explained. Although this amplification may be part of what the person meant, if it is not what they said, it shouldn't be bracketed by quotation marks.

For instance, the late Sir Denis Thatcher was quoted as saying, 'I do, and I also wash and iron them.' What did he mean? The quotation needs some explanatory words, such as, 'So who wears the trousers in the Thatcher household? "I do," said Sir Denis, "and I also wash and iron them."' This 21-word sentence makes use of two sets of quotation marks to delineate where the writer's contributions stop, and those of the person quoted begin.

Not for quotation

Quotation marks do have a life beyond flagging up direct quotes. They can be applied to words where a comment on the selected words is being implied, or those words have a hidden meaning. So if you write 'He had a rare and beautiful talent', this would be complimentary.

However, if you write, 'He had a "rare" and "beautiful" talent', then the quotation marks tell you that the person concerned possessed neither of these things.

Quotation marks also offer writers the ability to put distance between themselves and the subject they are writing about, without having to spell this out directly. For instance, 'It is claimed the revised timetable will "substantially improve" local rail services.' The quotation marks let you know that the writer thinks this is unlikely.

> **'Quotation marks offer writers the ability to put distance between themselves and the subject they are writing about.'**

Which means quotation marks should be used with care, as applied wrongly they can imply exactly the reverse of what the writer intended. Should you write glowingly about a restaurant that offers 'old world charm', the implication is that it has none at all. Read a column of private small ads and you will see this sort of thing all the time. Stuff like: 'Beautiful "top of the range" pushchair. Designed to "fold away easily", trimmed in "luxury fabrics" and in "fantastic condition".' The quotation marks are inappropriate, redundant (nothing is being quoted) and make a mockery of what's been written, because what they are is sarcasm in written form.

Punctuation and quotation

If a sentence includes a quote, I tend to use a comma immediately before the start of a quotation, as to my eye this reads more fluidly (He studied the painting then said, 'it's a fake'), but others disagree and do not, saying additional punctuation at this point is unnecessary. Whether you agree with them or me will depend on your personal preference.

Hyphens – the splice of life

There's a degree of subjective, personal choice when it comes to using the hyphen (-). With some words, such as 'cross country', you could join them up with a hyphen (cross-country) or leave them separate. Where they appear in dictionaries, you will find 'official' pro and anti stances for their use or omission, and will have to make a personal judgement on which you prefer.

Generally, the trend has been towards using them less, but hyphens are useful when inserted into compound words that would be hard to read if run together. What's a compound word? It's something that has a singular meaning but is named so because

'Hyphens are useful when inserted into compound words that would be hard to read if run together'

it joins a pair of words together, either completely, or in an abbreviated form. Technical terms sometimes fall into this category. One is 'hydro-pneumatic' (or, indeed, 'hydropneumatic', as both spellings are used). The term isn't the sort of thing you find every day, so is likely to cause some head scratching. The 'hydro' part of the word relates to water (as in 'fire hydrant'), and 'pneumatic' to gas. So 'hydro-pneumatic' technology uses both liquid and gas. Using a hyphen in the middle of this obscure word tells you that two things have been joined, and is easier on the eye.

There are plenty of commonly used words that are simply easier to read when hyphenated. One is 'pre-empt', which is visually unhappy when written as 'preempt', and harder to decipher as a result.

If you're adding a prefixed word ('pre', 'post', etc.) to something that starts with a capital letter, such as a name or a product, then this should always be hyphenated. So you'd have 'post-Churchill', not 'post Churchill', for example.

If you are adding a word to the beginning of something already hyphenated (or prefixing it), this will always get its own hyphen, as in 'non-drug-taking'.

Sometimes you can end up with a sentence that is overloaded with compound words that have been split up by hyphens, in which case it's worth rewriting as a means of tidying it up. So instead of something that reads, 'Private security guards have been accused of behaving like over-zealous vigilantes-cum-policemen,' you would produce something along the lines of, 'Private security guards are accused of exceeding their powers and behaving like vigilante-policemen.'

Famous names

There are millions of people with double-barrelled first and surnames. There are plenty of men named Jean-Claude and women called Tracy-Ann, and surnames like D'Arcy-Wigmore or Fotherington-Smythe. Equally there are plenty of Jean Claudes, Tracy Anns, D'Arcy Wigmores and Fotherington Smythes who get along without hyphenated names, so when such people are written about, this should always be checked.

Stressed

Adding hyphens can alter the stresses and meanings of words. For instance, write about going 'over the top', and the reader will infer that you're describing the process of climbing over something. If you write about going 'over-the-top', this infers that something has gone too far, or is too much.

Should you write about 'horse-trading', this is almost a generic term for haggling when negotiating a deal ('they engaged in the usual horse-trading over assets before signing the agreement'). On the other hand 'horse trading' involves the buying and selling of horses.

Dash it

If you wish to insert something into a sentence that thoroughly disrupts its flow, dashes can be used to achieve this. Here's an example: 'Only now – a decade after they were introduced – are the aid distribution policies becoming effective.'

Breaking up a sentence in this way at its mid point always requires a doubling up of hyphens or dashes, but the technique can be used with a single dash/hyphen at the end of a sentence if the words following it finish with a full stop. For example, 'Only now are the aid distribution policies becoming effective – a decade after they were introduced.'

- Apostrophes are used to contract words, or give them a possessive meaning (e.g. Joe's skateboard).

- Question marks should only be used in sentences where direct questions are being asked ('How are you?'). Indirect questions ('She asked why the room was being painted red.') appear without question marks.

- Commas break up phrases in a sentence where information is linked.

- Quotation marks should only be applied to what a person has actually said, when direct speech is being referred to.

- Quotation marks can also be used to flag up implied meanings of certain words. '"Interesting" does not describe the man.' suggests that he's really very dull.

- *Italicised* words are used for emphasis. They should be applied sparingly.

- Incorrect use of punctuation will make your work look amateurish.

- As with spelling, the rules of punctuation are not logical or uniform.

- If you're really struggling with an element of punctuation and need to get something finished, the problem can sometimes be bypassed by rewriting.

Chapter 8

GRAMMAR SCHOOL
Taking the grind from grammar

Isn't a chapter on basic grammatical terms and usage
a bit of an insult in a book like this? Surely anybody
reading it should be up to speed with these things?
Up to a point. There are plenty of very capable writers or
verbally articulate people who use adjectives, consonants,
adverbs and the like stylishly and effectively, without
necessarily knowing what these things are. They have
either forgotten which is which, or never really
took them on board when being taught.

Equally, there are plenty of writers with an encyclopaedic grammatical
knowledge and matching encyclopaedia-like prose styles.

It pays to understand grammar and style so that you can put them to
good use, but cramping your style for fear of making a mistake is a pity.
To help you avoid the worry, a basic nuts-and-bolts guide follows.

Nouns

Many hundreds of years ago – well, that's how it feels – I was taught in
primary school that a noun 'was the name of a person, place or thing'.
This childish mental short cut has stuck with me ever since, and means
that 'John', 'Simon' and 'Jean' are noun words. Likewise 'Mumbai' and
'China'. Cities and countries are both places. Things? How about
'chimney', 'diamond' and 'pocket'?

Unsurprisingly, there are numerous noun derivatives, including 'abstract nouns', which relate to things that don't exist in a tangible, physical sense, such as 'joy', 'misery', 'loyalty' and even 'history'.

Pronouns

These require separate description. These are words that stand in for nouns or noun phrases, which have already been specified earlier in the sentence or paragraph. For example: 'We collected all the golf balls and took them back to the club house,' instead of 'We collected all the golf balls and took the golf balls back to the clubhouse.' Pronouns such as 'me' and 'he' are known as 'personal pronouns', because they are specific to individuals. 'Mine' and 'theirs' are possessive pronouns, because they denote ownership or 'belonging to'. Interrogative pronouns add a questioning element (think 'what' and 'who', as in 'who will unblock the drain?'). Indefinite pronouns, such as 'anybody' and 'anything', provide less specific labels. There are other variations, if you want to look them up.

> 'Adjectives are noun-modifying words that describe a characteristic of a noun.'

Adjectives

Mostly, adjectives are noun-modifying words that describe a characteristic of a noun. So, when describing a 'green door', 'green' is the adjective, 'door' the noun. Adjectives can have an entirely abstract quality. Write, 'he had a beautiful mind', and 'beautiful' is the adjective that describes what this person's mind (the noun word) is like.

Verbs

These are 'doing' words. 'Go', 'run', 'decide' and 'repair' are verbs. In its most essential form, when a verb appears as a basic, descriptive word, which does not relate to a person, and which is used with the word 'to', it is known as an infinitive. Examples are 'to fly', 'to run', 'to sniff' and 'to annoy'. Change the tenses of these words in their conjugated forms ('flew', 'running', 'sniffed', 'annoys') and they are no longer infinitives. Their descriptive elements now stand alone, making the word 'to' redundant – if you wrote 'to flew' it wouldn't make a lot of sense.

Split infinitives

Like God, there's some argument over whether split infinitives exist, or if they do, whether they still matter. If you're writing for someone who believes that they are a bad thing, then identifying and eradicating them from your writing is probably a sensible course, and generally easy to achieve.

For believers, the sentence, 'They decided to never visit Aunt Mabel again' has a split infinitive, but 'They decided never to visit Aunt Mabel again' does not. How so? You are putting another word – 'never' between 'to' and the verb 'visit' in the first example, but not in the second.

Personally, I reckon the second version flows better, but don't find its predecessor offensive to read, and since many professional grammar watchers reckon split-infinitive-hating is a nonsense, would probably look at how well such a line worked on the page before deciding to edit it.

Adverbs

An adverb is a word that is added to a verb or adjective to qualify its meaning or the situation. Examples are 'quickly', 'finally', 'loudly'

Conjunctions

These are joining words, which marry up information. Examples include 'although', 'however' and 'because', as in, 'The train was late because of fallen leaves on the line.' Words like 'and' and 'but' also have a conjunctive function.

Double negatives

Groups of words that say 'no' twice. For instance, if you wrote 'it wouldn't not', you'd have committed a double negative crime. Why? Well, 'wouldn't' is an abbreviation of 'would not', so what has actually been written here is 'would not not'. Likewise 'he never said nothing'. If he 'never' said 'nothing', then he must have said something else instead (think about it). In this case, 'he never said anything' is the correct form.

Tension with tenses

One of the writer's perennial problems is sticking to the right time frame, or tense. You have three choices, but only two tenses that can be applied to them. Firstly, you can write about events that have taken place (past tense), are happening now or have yet to take place. These are regarded as being in the present tense, because in English, words like 'will' and 'shall' have combined present and future meanings. Some European languages, such as Spanish and French, contain words that do nothing but describe things that have yet to happen.

It's very easy to find that you've slipped from one period to another without meaning to, so that your work veers over several time zones when it should stick to one. How do you avoid this? Start by taking care not to switch halfway through an item where people are quoted in the past tense ('he said') to the present ('he says'). It's possible to blow a fuse in your brain thinking about this. Is a person talking in the present tense about something that took place in the past, or are their words in the past tense too? Should you write 'He says it should never have happened' or 'He said it should never have happened'? My default position is to write in the past tense, particularly when quoting people, because by definition what they said will be in the past when it's read by other people.

However, magazines and newspapers have different 'house styles' for this sort of thing, and may prefer quotes in the present tense, so I check first and write accordingly.

As for sticking with a particular tense throughout a piece of writing, this isn't always as simple as it seems. You could be cheerfully describing a historical event – let's say it's the publication 20 years ago of a paper on the love lives of insects – then quote someone involved with the project who said at the time, 'We predict this will revolutionise contemporary thinking about the sex drives of ants.'

All the words that came before make reference to laboratory technicians who 'had' conducted experiments, 'were' collecting data and 'took' risks. Suddenly you're saying that the ant-sex-drive person 'is proved right', and 'would go on to experiments involving horseflies', despite his words 'causing controversy'.

Given what he said has been reported as a direct quotation, you can't really change the words to, 'we predicted this would revolutionise', as this isn't what he said.

The choice is either to take his words out of direct quotation and paraphrase them: 'he *predicted*' (something he'd said in the past tense) 'they *would*' (present tense prediction about a future event) 'revolutionise', etc., or use the quote in full but suitably written around so that the rest of your story returns to the past tense.

Singles or doubles?

The confusion over using 'is' and 'are' is one of the more common problems with written English. It can occasionally fox busy professional writers, because a sentence that is wrong in this way can sometimes look and feel almost right.

This is particularly true when writing about businesses, companies and organisations. These bodies are mostly made up of more than one person, so it's not unnatural to think of them in the plural. Hence writing something along the lines of, 'Tata are planning to open a factory', 'Samsung are offering risk management training to their staff', or 'The World Health Organisation are launching a mass immunisation programme'. No, no and no again.

You should write in the singular: 'Tata *is* planning a new factory', 'Samsung *is* offering risk management training to *its* staff' and 'The World Health Organisation *is* launching a mass immunisation programme'. These bodies are all singular entities (note: I could also have written, 'each of these bodies is a singular entity'). When producing words about them, forget that they each employ a lot of individuals.

However, should you be writing about those individuals, the process has to be reversed. If applied to the Samsung quote, you might say: 'Staff at Samsung are being offered risk management training.' If you're working in the past tense then you'd write 'they *have been* offered...'.

For some people spotting this sort of thing isn't instinctive, but a mixture of practice and care should allow you to do so.

A few words about spelling

Since English spelling is contradictory and often illogical (e.g. words with identical pronunciations but different meanings and spellings, like 'there' and 'their', 'to', 'too' and 'two', etc.), you won't find a universal fix for getting things right.

However, there is a very useful method of deconstructing words, that will often take you to their correct spellings, or close enough to them that recourse to a computer's spell check facility, or a dictionary, will clear up any lingering errors. To do this you split these words into syllables.

Longer words in particular have a rhythm, which allows you to break them down into their constituent parts, or syllables. Generally, these are one, three or four letters long. If you don't want to interrupt the flow of writing by searching for a dictionary, then it's often possible to spell out a word in this way, highlighting it and coming back to it later for a final dictionary check. How about 'constituent' ('con-stit-u-ent') or intuition (in-tu-i-tion). Using this technique, even if you're a letter out, you can nail down the right version during editing.

This method is not entirely foolproof, and should not solely be relied on. For instance, in non-American English the pronunciation of the word 'theatre' is such that if it is split into syllables it comes out as 'the-at-er' not 'the-at-re' ('theater' is the word's American spelling). Nor will it be much help with something like 'fatigue'. It isn't pronounced 'fat-ig-ewe', nor is it spelt 'fateeg', despite its pronunciation.

However, for longer words with plenty of doubled-up letters, such as 'compassionate' (that's 'com-pass-ion-ate') it can work well. Taking words to pieces in this way helps your brain to think about their constructions, and to process them correctly. With practice, your eye will start to see words that simply don't look right – even if their spellings aren't wrong *per se*, but their contexts are.

Even if you have a disposition towards dyslexia, their shapes will begin to jump out at you when misspelled, or misplaced. For example if you saw a shop sign that said 'Dental Practise', you would recognise that the word 'practise' has been used in the wrong context: 'practise' is a verb, as in 'I'm bored stiff with practising the violin'; 'practice' is the noun.

Sounding off about vowels – vowels and spelling

Vowels are the letters 'a', 'e', 'i', 'o' and 'u', which, when spoken, involve the relatively free movement of air through the larynx and mouth (all the others, bar 'y' which has a stand-alone dual use, obstruct the passage of air in some way, and are called consonants).

With vowel sounds, one is the short, hard, flat 'phonetic' sound (the 'a' in words like 'attack'; and the 'e' in words like 'egg', etc.). Small children often use these sounds when first being taught how to read.

The other vowel sounds are longer and softer, so the letter 'a' is pronounced 'ay' (found in words like 'acorn'); 'e' becomes 'ee' (as in 'email'). Generally, this is triggered when a word with vowels has them separated by a single non-vowel letter, or actually grouped together. So 'utopia' is pronounced 'yoo-tope-ee-ah', since a single 't' keeps the 'u' and the 'o' apart while 'i' and 'a' sit alongside one another.

Contrast this with 'utter'. The pair of 't's' mean that the 'u' has the harder, phonetic 'uh' pronunciation, and the 'e' becomes 'eh'. You would never pronounce this word as 'ewe-teer'. So, knowing how a word is pronounced when spoken aloud will often help you spell it properly.

- **Nouns relate to people, places and things.**

- **Pronouns are words that stand in for nouns that have already been used in a sentence.**

- **Most adjectives describe the characteristics of nouns.**

- **Verbs are 'doing' words.**

- **Double negatives are groups of words that say 'no' twice. They should be avoided.**

- **It's often possible to 'hear' if a sentence is grammatically correct by reading it out loud.**

- **Everyone makes mistakes!**

- **Splitting words into syllables is often a helpful way of working out how they're spelt.**

Chapter 9

PITCH PERFECT
How to sell story ideas

This is a chapter which might seem irrelevant if you
have no journalistic aspirations, but if this is the case read
on, because it will help you to consolidate your
own ideas, their value and presentation. Thinking about
how you can make them appeal to others will
help you to judge their worth.

If you have journalistic story ideas, always find the appropriate person
to approach on the titles you think they best suit. In the UK, the
annually published *Writers' and Artists' Yearbook* is a thoroughly useful
medium for finding these people, and using an Internet search engine
will often put you on the right track.

However, don't assume any second-hand information is correct in
book form and especially on the Internet, which is stuffed with suspect
material. Remember, people change jobs, names are incorrectly spelt,
and so on. So before pitching, phone the journal and ask who the
arts/gardening/fashion editor is. Check their exact job title, how their
name is spelt and the address.

At this stage, you don't have to talk with the person concerned, if you
explain what you want to the receptionist, and ask that they supply the
information rather than put you through. Usually I'm completely
upfront with receptionists about being a journalist who wants to send
the person some ideas, and am rarely fobbed off. If you sound vague
and shifty, they may balk at helping you.

Was it me?

Commissioning editors tend to be busy and have particular niches and areas they need written material for. They have often limited budgets and people in charge of them who will want certain things commissioned or written in a particular way. They sometimes reject ideas their subordinates would like to see used. These might include yours.

Good commissioning editors are pleasant to deal with, decisive and helpful. They know what they want – or don't want – and can explain why clearly. They might see potential in an idea and want to find out if you can develop it in a way that perhaps hadn't occurred to you. These people understand just how nerve wracking it can be to cold call someone to get work by offering them stories – even if you've dealt with them before. Others do not, or are working under such tremendous pressure that they haven't got time for empathy, particularly if they're dealing with someone who isn't part of their stable of regular writers. A few have social skills that make dealing with them akin to receiving a blow to the cranium with a crowbar.

> 'Good commissioning editors are pleasant to deal with, decisive and helpful.'

Freelance for long enough and along the way you will encounter rudeness, indifference, arrogance and carelessness, but these traits are found in all sorts of people in many walks of life. Generally this sort of behaviour isn't personal, and if you want to prosper as a freelance writer, remaining gracious and moving on is the best policy for dealing with it.

Gulp!

Even after more than a decade-and-a-half of freelancing, I often find the pitching process gut-churning, and have to work hard at not getting tongue-tied or underselling my ideas. Confidence is hard to fake, and because the work is so personal – it's coming from an individual, not somebody from X magazine or Y paper – when people say 'no', it's sometimes hard to move on.

One secret to reducing writer's stress is to shrug and walk away from your idea, even if it is of obvious genius, if nobody else is interested. Perhaps it can be amended, revived later, or adapted, but plugging away at something that is not going to happen is a waste of time.

Timing

When following up an introductory letter, story ideas and (hopefully) examples of what you've already done, timing your 'Hello, it's me!' call is important.

If you're speaking to someone working on a weekly magazine that appears on a Thursday, calling mid morning on Tuesday won't endear you. He or she will probably be in the middle of a press day, when the next issue is being put together, and talking to a writer touting for work will not be a priority. Better to get in touch on publication day, or perhaps the day after. If your intended publication appears on a weekend, Fridays and Mondays are likely to be less hectic.

> **'When following up an introductory letter, timing your "Hello, it's me!" call is important.'**

If you are a little unsure about how the person's first or surnames are pronounced, check with the telephone receptionist before you ask them to put you through. After that, find out if you're speaking to the right person before launching into your pitch.

Have the list of ideas to hand, and once you've established that you're speaking to the right person, ask if he or she has seen them, and if not, offer to re-send. Often you'll be asked to email, even if they haven't seen cuttings.

Not like this

During my tenure as a commissioning editor, the newspaper supplement I worked for ran a piece about motor scooters. One day the phone rang and a voice said, 'That scooter story – did you *pay* someone to write it?'

I said the piece was the work of our office trainee and asked who wanted to know. The owner of the voice replied that he was a specialist scooter journalist, the story was utter rubbish, and since he could do much better, I really ought to employ him instead.

As it happened, the story was not rubbish, but had it been, telling the person who'd sanctioned it was unlikely to endear this bearer of bad tidings to him. Perhaps the caller was trying to demonstrate his self-belief and honesty. What he demonstrated was something else entirely.

Managing not to lose my temper, I asked the scooter expert to write in with a list of ideas and some examples of his work. What arrived were some mediocre cuttings and an ideas-free letter, written by hand on a sheet of lined A4 paper with two binder holes punched in one side. Its author said he was 'sorry' if his call had upset me ('upset' was not the word), but it was important to point out unprofessional writing – a subject in which he was clearly well versed.

> '**A good idea lazily presented is likely to be rejected, misunderstood or ignored.**'

Strangely, he never wrote for my supplement, but the trainee he'd maligned kept practising and is now a working journalist.

Presentation

With established outlets I tend to pitch by email. Often I draw together several ideas, and work hard at finding a way of writing about them that neatly encapsulates what they're about before hitting my email's 'send' button. A good idea lazily presented is likely to be rejected, misunderstood or ignored. If it can't be made to sound exciting to the person you hope will commission it, what chance does it have of interesting readers? Does it fit in with the stories already being run by the title you've approached?

Once, after I'd sent some ideas to the editor of a newspaper property supplement, she asked me what single element of each meant that people would want to read them. I reread the submissions and, in most cases, couldn't actually say. I knew they had potential, and that they contained the kernels of good ideas, but hadn't thought them through completely.

As a writer, you may find the detail of a story is sometimes more interesting than the hook by which you hope it will be sold, but it needs that hook to get written in the first place. You should always be able to say 'people will read this because…'.

As for having your ideas ripped off – this is actually very rare. But remember, if you see potential in a subject, others might already have done so.

Soliciting

Generally speaking, I do not recommend sending unsolicited material. Mostly, such things are received with a groan, frequently do not fit with their intended title's house style, and are rarely used.

This isn't exclusively true. As an aspirant journalist, keen to prove that I could write for a weekly magazine with a celebrity interview slot, I persuaded a famous lady newspaper columnist, the late Jean Rook, to be a subject. She had a fearsome

> '**Generally speaking, I do not recommend sending unsolicited material.**'

reputation, so I made sure she knew that I hadn't been commissioned, and that the story might never appear, so I wouldn't get into trouble if it didn't. Rook must have taken pity on me, since she gave me her time.

I sent in the copy, having first looked very hard at the style of its intended slot, and when the magazine's next planned interview fell through, my piece was the right length and could fill the gap. It was the first of many I was to write for them, but only because what I had offered was something they needed, in the style that was required.

Give them what they want

Writing great screeds of material about something outside a title's comfort zone will probably be a waste of your time and theirs, and could well alienate you from them should your ideas and their requirements gel later on.

> **'Anybody with a professional track record will view "on spec" with distrust.'**

Giles Chapman is a freelance writer, and one-time editor of *Classic & Sports Car* magazine, a glossy monthly that often features stories about exotic old cars. He recalls people sending in poems about their favourite ancient motors. These had nothing to do with the structure and dynamic of the title itself.

You might find yourself being asked to write something 'on spec'. Anybody with a professional track record will view 'on spec' with distrust, as potentially it's a great way to waste time and be mucked about.

Recently, I was foolish enough to produce some words on spec for a literary magazine that I liked very much. One editor rated my copy and wanted to use it, but another, who turned out to be his boss, did not, and spiked the story.

When I asked what I might do in order to change the piece so it would meet his criteria, this man said he rejected so many on-spec stories that he 'couldn't remember', and was too busy to check, but I was welcome to try and guess, and rewrite it with no guarantee that it would be used.

There are appropriate words to describe this approach. Sadly they are inappropriate to print here, but anyone who mucks people about like this should be avoided. Had he been serious about the piece, he would have looked at my story and asked for specific changes.

Some people find saying 'no' very difficult, and rather than doing so he was prepared to let me waste time chasing shadows.

No matter how keen you are to get into print, or want your work to appear in a particular title, do not go down this road. If you are asked to write an on-spec item, get a clear brief from the person involved, explaining what he or she wants, and stick to it.

Look before you leap

Not understanding what a title is seeking, and trying to give it something else, is a common failing among writers with journalistic ambitions. Murdo Morrison is familiar with this syndrome. He edits *Flight International*, a highly respected, specialist journal. With readers in a hundred and ninety countries, it covers a huge range of business, social and technical stories involving both civil and military aviation. And yet it doesn't deviate from its core interests.

> '**Not understanding what a title is seeking, and trying to give it something else, is a common failing.**'

'It's amazing the number of people who pitch features who appear never to have opened a copy of the magazine,' he says. 'We get people who say, "I've got a great story about a flight I made in a Piper (light aircraft) over the Andes," and you think, "Fine, but we don't do that sort of stuff."'

He has a simple mantra: 'Know your market. Know the magazine you want to write for, and read it, so that you know what pushes its buttons.'

Morrison says that this means looking at story lengths, particular areas of content that are popular, and writing styles. 'If a magazine has a lot of one-page, 1,000-word features, don't go pitching a 5,000-word novelette.'

He says anyone with no track record pitching an on spec idea to *Flight International* will have a tough job getting past his 'initial scepticism'. Morrison also has the luxury of editing a magazine people want to write for, which gives him the choice of using the best writers in their fields. These are people who've proved to him they can deliver professionally.

He thinks people who want to emulate them can sometimes develop working relationships with commissioning editors 'by starting small, writing the odd little snippet', and using these stories to build up experience and a cuttings file. If the work is good, it can sometimes lead to bigger jobs.

Morrison thinks freelancers tread a fine line when dealing with the editors who control whether their work and ideas are used. 'Being confident enough to push when trying to sell your stuff (is fine), but don't antagonise. Who's editing the magazine? Who's writing the cheque? Being pestered to take a story you don't want is like somebody insisting you need double glazing.'

Good impressions

When using outside writers, Morrison says he is 'pathetically impressed' by those who make an extra effort not only to give him what he wants, but also other things that make his life easier. 'If the copy is due on a Monday, get it in on the previous Friday. Effectively I'm also *Flight*'s features editor, and if I can hand over a story early, that makes me look good.

'You could perhaps suggest headlines, where we could source pictures, or offer to help supply them. If the art editor doesn't know where to start, that's sure to go down well.'

Delivery

Offering one story then delivering another is also to be avoided. This happens surprisingly frequently, and is a great way to generate alienation and poverty through lack of work. In my commissioning days I was offered a news item about a motorcycle with a plastic fuel tank that would, under certain circumstances, melt.

This came from the editor of a motorcycle magazine, and I asked for a 300-word news story, which he agreed to provide. What appeared was a 750-word road test. Buried near the end of this tract was a paragraph that raved about the machine's capabilities, 'despite an unimportant problem'. It did not say what that problem was.

> **'Offering one story then delivering another is also to be avoided.'**

We never ran motorcycle road tests of this length, it wasn't a news story, and it wasn't about the melting fuel tank. Otherwise it was spot-on. Perhaps the author had decided that the bike's makers would no longer advertise in his magazine if the piece he'd originally promised appeared, and he'd tried to bury it – but why did he offer the thing to start with?

A pain to explain

There are plenty of people who know about things but can't really write about them, don't seem to learn where they're going wrong and struggle along selling the odd piece to outlets that never seem to employ them again. A newspaper arts editor told me how she used to bemoan some freelancers who came up with 'brilliant' ideas, but were always so wide of the mark in terms of what they actually wrote, that she would turn them down, thinking, 'Damn! I wish someone else had thought of that.'

If you think a piece is worth 1,000 words and the commissioning editor asks for 500, tough. It's your job to make those words shine.

Don't be tempted to overwrite either. Editors often think in page shapes (and even with the advance of Internet publishing, this still applies). Whatever the medium, print or electronic, these are holes with limited space for words and pictures. If you produce 650 words for a 500-word slot, on the basis that the person who commissioned you can have the extra as a gift, and cut back as they see fit, you're just giving them extra work, which was expected of you. This will not make you popular.

Study the publication for style details before you start work. Do its writers work in the past or present tense ('she said' or 'she says')? When people are directly quoted, are single or double quotation marks used? If commas, full stops, etc. appear with them, are they used before ('hello,') or after ('hello',)? Different publications have their own 'house styles', and if you've taken the trouble to work out what these style points are, then people who matter might be pleasantly surprised.

> **'Study the publication for style details before you start work.'**

Finally, look closely at what is being done to your work when it appears. If it keeps getting heavily edited this isn't a good sign, and it's worth finding out why, and amending what you do accordingly. I worked with several writers who clearly never did this, repeatedly made the same mistakes, and often complained the loudest when I asked for changes.

Generally, it was the most able, confident writers who adapted to what was asked of them, although their copy retained the original spark that made it attractive to start with, and when changes were requested, they were made quickly and accurately.

Tough luck

Establishing yourself as a credible writer will be difficult, especially if you are trying to break into the business from outside the conventional route of further education, journalism college, etc.

It's far from impossible, but as we've seen, in most areas of writing there are already plenty of people who can nearly do it, can't do it very well, so brutalise words on a regular basis, or think they're literary geniuses, and don't take the trouble to learn their craft. Most commissioning editors know who the good people are in their given fields, know most of the rest, and will be used to approaches from wannabes who could swell the latter's ranks still further. So they may not greet you with much enthusiasm or confidence. Proving them wrong, with a mix of professionalism and clever ideas won't be easy (even getting the chance to do so will be tough), but the only way to find out if you can is to try.

- Always find a single, strong hook for a story idea ('I should write this because…').

- Thoroughly read the title you hope to write for.

- Make sure you can offer stories they're likely to want, not that you think they should have.

- When contacting potential outlets, make sure you're speaking to the appropriate person, that you know how to pronounce their name, etc.

- Do not call on press day!

- Be certain you can deliver what you claim. If circumstances change, liaise with the person who's asked for the story, and seek guidance.

- Do not overwrite.

- Find ways to add value to your work (picture sourcing suggestions, etc.).

- Be flexible. If changes are asked for, accept them with good grace.

- Self confidence is a good attribute. Arrogance is not.

- Meet, or beat, deadlines.

Chapter 10

LIFE AS A FREELANCE WRITER
Self-help for self-starters

The idea of writing for a living is an appealing
one for many people, and doing this on a freelance
basis is perhaps the most attractive of all. The work is
potentially varied and creative, and perhaps allows you to
indulge personal interests and passions. You escape
from office politics and have more control over
how your time is spent.

Well, that's the theory, and up to a point it can be the reality too, but by its nature, writing is a solitary process – whichever area of it attracts you – and writing at home can be a very lonely and isolating experience indeed.

Many established freelancers, especially ex staff journalists, try to find titles that want them to work on site from time to time as a way of spending some of their time in a professional working environment, a luxury book authors often do not have.

If you're not busy writing and researching, then you're generating ideas and trying to sell them, and will have to get used to setbacks, rejections and simply being ignored by busy people who need you less than you need them.

You will have become used to work cycles that seem to go from famine to feast, when you are working through a fat stack of commissions, but are reluctant to turn down others that arrive at the same time for fear that you won't be offered jobs in the future.

The most successful freelance writers tend to have decent social skills, full contacts books, and a flexible approach (even if they're specialists in particular subjects), always finding new outlets for their skills and knowledge and being prepared to re-invent themselves.

Those who have learnt to successfully navigate the freelance writing world have a lot to teach anyone with similar aspirations about attitudes and approaches to their craft, as much as the craft itself.

> **'The most successful freelance writers tend to have decent social skills, full contacts books, and a flexible approach.'**

Giles Chapman and Jon Courtenay Grimwood earn their livings writing a mix of books, feature and specialist articles.

Courtenay Grimwood is a columnist for the *Guardian*, and has wide-ranging experience as a contributor to magazines including glossy men's lifestyle magazines *Maxim* and *Esquire*, and women's titles such as *New Woman*. He's also a science fiction novelist, and came to writing from a background in book publishing and editing.

'I had a small son, needed a job that allowed for school holidays and half terms. I volunteered for redundancy, went freelance and lucked into writing for the *Guardian*,' he says.

Chapman also has extensive experience as an editor, columnist, corporate copy writer and even obituarist. His specialism is motoring, but he has always brought a wider journalistic sensibility to the subject, because he wants people who aren't necessarily interested in it to read and enjoy his words, too.

Although he and Courtenay Grimwood operate in very different areas, the way they work has a lot in common.

Back of the class

At school, Chapman was a voracious reader of car magazines, 'probably in Chemistry, waiting for the board rubber to bounce off my head… I'd been reading [them] since I was 12, really absorbing the data in a solitary child kind of way.'

As a teenager he secured a job 'as a glorified tea boy' for an automotive archive in London, where he had just moved and initially had no friends ('This is not my life as a weirdo,' he stresses). Chapman thought of ideas for the magazines he loved reading, and began spending weekends at his employer's office researching and writing. 'What I did was shamelessly copy the style of what was in the magazines I read. I'd think, "What are they likely to want?"'

Chapman describes himself then as 'quite green', and the magazines he coveted as 'distant kingdoms', but he'd tapped into a natural journalistic sensibility by finding ways to fill gaps in the magazines with material they wanted. Commissions became ever more frequent, and eventually he was headhunted by *Classic & Sports Car* magazine as an editorial assistant, where he learned every aspect of writing, editing and putting a magazine together.

'I'd do the readers' letters, editing them right down. I'd write the contents page and things with lots of detail, but people read all these bits and pieces, and I'd try to find ways of making them interesting.'

Chapman learned his trade by a mix of hands-off guidance, intuition and practice. 'Some of my intros [opening paragraphs] were just appalling. When I was writing features I was trying a little too hard.' This came in part from wanting to inject interest in often necessarily formulaic stories such as buyers' guides. 'I started to notice what other intros were like on other things. I was allowed to learn on the job.'

Gatekeeping

Chapman wrote headlines and 'standfirsts', the short bursts of text that introduce articles, becoming obsessed with making these readable and eye-catching. The need to attract readers and make them keep turning the magazine's pages became 'the stuff of life'.

He was to take on a variety of jobs with the magazine, including staff writer and assistant editor. Along the way he managed freelance writers, briefing them and editing their work. In the process his critical faculties 'took a quantum leap'.

'I'd think, "Is this story any good? If I'm bored subbing it, will readers be bored? If it has a really left-field spin, and we have a fairly conservative readership, will they get it?"'

A different perspective

Jon Courtenay Grimwood thinks his approach to work is in part formed by dyslexia.

'To be honest, being dyslexic gives you a stronger interest in language, and how it's put together,' he says. Not always 'seeing' written words, and so not automatically spotting when they're incorrectly spelt or written down, has meant that he's had to study them with a more forensic eye. Likewise sentences, which are, he says, 'just building blocks you can take apart'.

Dyslexia does not exclude a person from writing well, even brilliantly, and Courtenay Grimwood long ago came to regard it as irrelevant to his work. Dyslexics are often unusually articulate and develop a strong verbal sense for the things that make good sentence structures. This can feed back into their writing, once they have surmounted the challenge of making that writing ordered and legible.

Courtenay Grimwood says learning to type 'changed my life'. The arrival of word processors that allowed corrections to be made on screen rather than on paper was also liberating.

As someone who went through school attending 'remedial' writing classes and today often finds reading back his own handwriting hard work, his formative experiences strike a chord with me. Learning to type meant I no longer had to force my mind to slow down when writing, resulting in erratic sentences with words missed out or repeated, as it wandered while waiting as my pen laboriously worked to catch up.

Self-help

Chapman spent a decade changing from 'a shy, spavined teenager' into an accomplished magazine editor and writer, before going freelance, and applying what he'd learned to stories for a broad range of titles.

'The one thing I wanted to do was write for the daily newspapers. I was quite well placed to do this, but felt I had an awful lot to learn.'

This meant finding story 'hooks' that would pull in readers who normally wouldn't look at a piece about cars. In specialist magazines, readers being interested in the subject was a given, but when writing for papers, Chapman adapted his 'turn the page' sensibilities by finding people-led, 'colour' stories, which involved cars, rather than writing about cars in detailed, reverential terms.

In this guise he wrote about a day in the life of a city vehicle pound, the people who worked there, and those who came to retrieve their towed-away vehicles. Another piece was on the surprising contents of drivers' glove boxes. These were stories with broad popular appeal from a writer with a specialist background.

Feedback

Courtenay Grimwood reckons the disciplines imposed by journalism help his book writing. 'You work to set deadlines and set word amounts. It's structured.' He enjoys working to briefs, and does not think that these cramp him creatively. 'You learn to write a 2,000-word feature, top and tail it, provide two pieces of expert advice, three lots of statistics and some stuff in the middle. Most people who write novels can't plan to save their lives,' says Courtenay Grimwood, who grew used to filing five or six features every month.

He reckons the thought processes involved in journalism strip away the 'displacement activity' elements sometimes tied up with the more obviously creative process of producing a novel, so that when he delivers a book it's on time and the right length.

'I know people who have been seven years late with books. Many are six months to a year late. They have absolutely no comprehension that they might have missed their publishing slot and messed up the marketing people.'

Fashion victims

The capacity to think laterally about subjects, find new angles, and different areas to write about are meat and drink to many freelancers, and it's this constant churning of material that makes their working lives interesting, as well as occasionally stressful. Employing a freelance journalist's capacity to adapt will help any writer's work.

'You've got to keep exploring new fields and looking for the next thing.'

'You've got to keep exploring new fields and looking for the next thing,' says Chapman. This includes finding new outlets for work, and accepting that some long-standing contacts may wither. Chapman recalls one newspaper where he 'had a really good run, but suddenly it went cold'.

Courtenay Grimwood thinks both writers and subjects have finite lives in a particular form.

'Something can be enormously fashionable, sexy or whatever dreadful word you want to use, and two years later you can't sell it to save your life. I lucked out on the Internet. A lot of what I wrote in the *Guardian* and *The Independent* explained what the Web was, and it was great writing this stuff, but suddenly everybody had wireless [Internet] technology in their homes.' This meant that most of the people who had wanted to know how this technology worked did so, and no longer wanted to read about it.

'As a journalist or a novelist, you have to reinvent yourself every four or five years, or people think "he only writes about one thing",' says Courtenay Grimwood.

This requires time to stand back and examine where changes need to be made and how work can be developed. When a writer is busy there is often very little time to do this, and when he or she is not, the need to pay bills often forces that person towards familiar territory and contacts, rather than trying to develop fresh outlets, which can take up valuable working time without a guarantee of success. Nevertheless, finding ways to do this is part of the job.

Recycling

However, this does not mean somebody who has earned a name as a specialist writer has to completely walk away from their primary subject, but they need to adapt it to changing demands. Perversely, the constant reinvention process can mean unearthing, repackaging and reselling ideas that have been used successfully in the past, and finding new outlets for them.

'All journalists have about six stories they reuse,' reckons Chapman. 'Subjects are going to come back again. Think of Jonathan Glancey, who writes about architecture for the *Guardian*. How many pieces has he done on futurism?'

How clever of you

Chapman reckons that commissioning editors like to feel they have 'some ownership' of the ideas being offered to them. This generally means these will be changed in some way before being accepted. A story involving 10 unusual items will be expanded to 25, an interview piece with five interviewees will require commentary from a sixth person suggested by the commissioning editor, etc.

Chapman describes saleable stories as those which have an 'I didn't know that' factor.

'I don't have a high opinion of where I should be,' he says. 'If my business card said "populist and vulgarian", I wouldn't mind particularly. The excitement is the same as it ever was. I'm a reader myself, and think I know what other people will read.'

Courtenay Grimwood thinks professional writing is a mixture of art and trade. 'You learn to write the way you build a house. Make the foundations, learn to lay bricks, install the electrics. Almost everybody can write to a level that is functional.'

- **Freelance writing is a tough business. Everyone involved with it is expendable and replicable.**

- **The other side of career self-determination is that working from home can be very isolating. Are you prepared to live with this?**

- **A flexible mindset about ideas and outlets is essential.**

- **Things change. Cherished ideas go out of fashion. Be prepared to change what you write and who you write it for.**

- **However, some hardy perennial ideas can make a comeback. Keep a list, and have a notebook to hand to jot down thoughts that can develop into stories.**

Chapter 11

FREELANCE JOURNALISM
A working life

Nicole Swengley is a London-based freelance feature writer specialising in 'lifestyle' journalism (subjects like design and property), contributing to the *Financial Times*, *The Times* and the *London Evening Standard*. She attributes having the self-discipline to work from home to 'fear' and the need to clear bills and meet mortgage repayments.

Swengley says that keeping set hours of work provides a structure for the day. 'Personally, I like to get to my desk early – about 8am – although I have been known to start at 7am or even 5.30am for a really pressing deadline. I will then work until 1pm, when I stop for a sandwich and listen to Radio 4's *World at One* programme. I'll return to my desk around 1.30pm and carry on for a few hours, then go for a swim or a walk round the local park before returning to my desk for a couple of hours more. I generally knock off at 6pm and there are often press events to attend between 6.30pm and 8.30pm. I rarely work after supper if I'm at home in the evening because I like to have time to wind down from the day.'

Inevitably, working days don't always follow exactly the same pattern. When Swengley isn't researching and writing, she can be attending meetings or be away from home for interviews or press events. She occasionally goes into newspaper offices to work.

'At home I work in a dedicated room so that I'm not distracted by all the domestic chores that need doing elsewhere in my apartment. I try to meet friends in the evenings, rather than at lunchtime, to minimise the temptation of whiling away the afternoon in a café or wine bar,' she says.

'I find that it's important to have at least one commission in hand so that there is always another job to move on to when the last one is finished. Staring at a blank commissions book is an open invitation to slack off!'

She says that newspapers 'are in a constant state of flux', and commissioning editors change regularly. 'Hopefully, you have produced work to a high enough standard to survive a change of commissioning editor. It's wise to check whether a new editor's approach will remain the same as their predecessor and, if not, to establish how you can tailor your ideas to suit.'

Swengley tries to keep in touch with editors who've moved on, as this can sometimes lead to more work with the titles they've joined – although this doesn't always pay off.

'It's important not to keep all your eggs in one basket and to add fresh outlets by approaching publications for which you have not worked previously. This also helps avoid the problem of getting stale.

'When I hit a quiet patch I find it helps to look back at my personal press cuttings book to see who I was working for a year or two back,' she says. This is something many writers do to refresh their thoughts. It's also a good way of re-evaluating work, and keeping up standards.

'If I haven't worked for that publication for a while then I may contact them again with new ideas,' she says. 'It's also worth visiting a good newsagent to remind yourself just how many newspapers and magazines there are to write for and to make the effort to contact the ones you like, having thought up fresh or new ideas to offer them.'

How does she deal with interviewees who, on seeing the words she's produced say, 'I never said that?'

'I can truthfully say that no one I've interviewed has ever said this to me. Perhaps this is because I try to be scrupulous about quotes. I do not believe it is professional to alter what someone has said to fit the angle or theme of a story.

'When I conduct interviews I prefer to scribble notes in my own personal version of shorthand rather than use a tape recorder. One reason for this is that I find it quicker and easier to write from my notes rather than transcribing a taped conversation and, as I read through my notes, I find I hear their voice in my head. In any case, some interviewees do not like to be taped.

'If the whole piece is to be presented as first-person quotes from the interviewee, and entirely in their own words, then I may very occasionally email my draft to them before filing the copy, so that they can read through what they said before it is published. It's rare to find that they wish to change anything and, in any case,

'It's important not to keep all your eggs in one basket and to add fresh outlets by approaching publications for which you have not worked previously.'

it's my view that if they wish to amend what they originally said then, in certain circumstances, they should have the opportunity to do so.'

Nervous interviewees quoted in general stories often express fears about their words being taken out of context or being misunderstood, but giving them control over what goes on the page is something Swengley never does. After all, the person being interviewed is not paying for her services. Also, some interviewees do not understand what makes good writing, and there's a small risk that they will decide to alter what they've said or start asking for changes to the thrust of the piece.

'As a compromise, when asked to show copy, I sometimes offer to go through the story over the phone, which means the interviewee is given the direct quotations they've made and knows that they're not being misquoted, while I still decide on the structure of the story.'

Swengley maintains that her approach is 'very different from agreeing with the interviewee in advance that they will have "copy approval" – something I never do – because it is still up to me whether or not to include any amendments before publication.'

- Self discipline in terms of how working days are structured is essential.

- A dedicated work area will separate you from any household distractions.

- Socialising in the evenings rather than at lunchtime helps avoid the temptation to put off work.

- Working for a wide range of outlets means that your income isn't dependent on a few titles.

- Do not give 'copy approval' to interviewees, but occasionally you may choose to show them what has been written, if the story is entirely in first-person quote form and attributed to them.

- Looking at old stories is a good way to generate or revive ideas.

Chapter 12

LEGAL AID
Writing and the law

We live in a litigious age. Postal workers struggle under the weight of solicitors' letters as never before, and people seem ever keener to resort to the law if they feel wronged. So anybody who goes into print risks finding themselves on the receiving end of someone's legal ire, perhaps for reasons of genuine grievance, as a means of shutting down unfavourable comment, or as a method of making money. This chapter provides a general overview, rather than a detailed examination of the law as it affects writers.

Freelance journalist and journalism trainer, Richard Sharpe, has a stark warning. 'People have become more litigious in the last 10–15 years,' he says. 'The number of solicitors' letters is as high, or higher, than it has ever been.' Sharpe is co-owner of Editorial Training Consultants. This UK-based company's name is self-explanatory, and its clients include big publishing houses such as EMAP and Haymarket.

Understandably, Sharpe concentrates on British law as it applies to writers, but much of what he says has a wider resonance, whether you're in Ashford, England, Agra, India, or Auckland, New Zealand. He suggests that in Britain, the emergence of legal practices offering to take cases on a 'no win, no fee' basis has had a big impact. 'A lot of people who wouldn't have been able to afford [to sue] for libel can because of the no win, no fee rule,' he says.

He thinks changes to the British Civil Code – known as the Woolf Reforms and intended to tidy up legal terminology and make the law more accessible, faster and cheaper – have also played a part here. So the law is now less impenetrable, and in theory at least, less ruinously expensive (although often the reverse is still true), and some people are now more willing to risk using it, or have been encouraged to do so.

Power of three

'There are three areas of media law at least that most hacks should get their heads round,' says Sharpe. These are copyright infringement, *sub judice* and defamation.

When answering allegations of defamation, writers and publishers sometimes use the 'Reynolds Defence'. To 'defame' someone is to damage their good name (in the literal sense, the word means the removal of a person's fame. They have been 'de-famed'). Generally, 'slander' is perceived by legal experts as the verbal equivalent of defamation.

The Reynolds Defence precedent arose from a legal spat between former Irish prime minister (or Taoseach) Albert Reynolds and *The Sunday Times* newspaper, which claimed 'qualified privilege' for what it had printed about him.

This means that defendants claim their story is in the public interest. *The Sunday Times'* defence, according to Sharpe, was 'we're not saying this is true. What we're saying is that we've done a good bit of journalism to back it up.'

The case ground through the judicial system until the English Law Lords decided in favour of the newspaper, which had to prove its story told people something they needed to know, ventilated serious allegations and information, that these came from creditable sources, that what they said was verifiable, and that steps had been taken to confirm this. The tone of what had been written, whether the story's subject had been given a right of reply, and the circumstances of publication, including its timing, also had to be considered.

The acid test was whether the story had been written to tell readers something useful, or to damage its subject. Was it informative or accusatory? It was decided that *The Sunday Times* piece passed this test.

Opinion formers

Anybody writing potentially contentious material should consider that a degree of personal interpretation of law by judges or magistrates will effect how it's deployed, and that their views on what constitutes 'public interest' might not concur with the wider legal establishments' (interpretation of the law varies, even though the parameters for that interpretation are often fixed). This is true no matter how hard-worked, checked-out or honestly intended a story is, but the clearer the note taking, the more thorough the cross-referencing and attribution, the better.

File not forget

In the UK, anybody who feels they've been libelled in print has a 12-month window in which to seek legal redress (on the Internet, there's a 12-month period from when it is first spotted), so it is actually worth keeping notes for about three years.

'Making individual job files and keeping them in month order is a good rule-of-thumb method.'

You might write something and be asked to justify an arcane point in your story 18 months later, when you've long forgotten much of what it contained. Some solicitors trawl through the most obscure publications looking for potentially actionable words. So, being able to reach into a file, check and confirm who said what is important, as is being able to say where written pieces of information used in your story originated.

Consider the effort expended in organising and filing as an insurance policy. It will be time well spent if somebody claims you've misquoted them, that you got your facts wrong or lied. As for how you file, people have different systems, but making individual job files and keeping them in month order is a good rule-of-thumb method.

This doesn't just apply to working journalists. You might only be writing for a limited local audience, or perhaps putting something in a letter, but if the subject is contentious and involves others who could claim that what you've written damages their reputations, the same laws will apply to you. The ability to back up your assertions with physically verifiable information may not prevent a solicitor's letter plopping onto your doormat, but could rapidly neutralise its contents.

Not to be missed

For the recipients of such correspondence, Richard Sharpe's advice is simple: 'Don't get worried, but act swiftly. Unless you've done something stupid there's normally a defence.' He thinks human nature means that people are tempted to put legal letters 'to the bottom of the pile. They then write you another letter and the solicitor gets another £250. In many instances you haven't broken the law. All you've done is upset some geezer who's got access to a lawyer.'

What if said geezer has cause for his upset? 'If you've made a cock-up, put your hand up – through a solicitor,' reckons Sharpe. 'The day you get a problem sorted out is the day you can walk away from it.'

Private lives

One defence a professional writer has against accusations of defamation is that of 'fair comment'. If he or she can prove that what they have written is an honestly held opinion, expressed without malice, a public interest element is also often applied here.

This explains why politicians and many public figures rarely sue if on the receiving end of less than flattering write-ups in the press, when these come under the heading of 'comment'. However, it's one thing to say that a movie actor's stage debut is a disaster, if that's what you think, but quite another to suggest that he's having an affair, when there's no hard evidence to support this, and your primary motive is a personal dislike of the man's work.

If untrue, or unprovable, the latter could leave you open to accusations of libel, and be perceived as an invasion of the person's privacy. Sharpe says that moves by the European Court of Human Rights in this area are leading to a change in emphasis in UK courts. 'There's a significant shift taking place between freedom of expression and "public interest" and privacy. The shift is towards privacy,' he says.

Copyright

Referring to other people's written work, as long as it's credited and attributed, is generally fine, provided this is done in the context of something you've written, or you're writing about it (in the case of a report or study, for instance). However, simply lifting material and regurgitating it as if it was something you had produced is a form of stealing and potentially a breach of someone else's copyright – although proving this is often difficult.

'People need to get their heads round copyright. Just because you can cut and paste from a computer or use a photocopier, doesn't mean to say that you should,' says Sharpe.

The Web has made this sort of thing easier still, and this has provided greater temptations to the light-fingered or naïve. This is particularly true in the case of photographs, cartoons and illustrations. Copyright for them is less abstract than that for words or ideas, so permission will need to be sought and very possibly payment made.

Branded

We've dealt elsewhere with the occasionally problematic use of trademarked names as if they have generic meanings (such as 'hoovering' for vacuum cleaning, 'Hoover' being a trademarked name), but generations of solicitors have swelled their bank balances by writing letters in legalese, defending their client's good names from 'inappropriate' use, breach of copyright, etc. Should you receive one of these letters, how you react to it will depend on whether it's intended to rap your knuckles and apply a bit of courtroom terror, or is threatening potentially expensive legal action.

Not now

The term *sub judice*, which has a dictionary definition of 'under consideration', is often heard in the context of writing and journalism, but Sharpe thinks that it's widely misunderstood. 'This is when a thing is under judgement, where an official process is going on, and nothing you write about it should influence those who will see [your words],' he says.

Contempt-of-court rules can also apply here, and trials have been abandoned because things have been written about them in advance that are perceived as being likely to impact on their eventual outcomes. 'It's dangerous to introduce new material or speculate on the value or variety of evidence,' says Sharpe.

However, this doesn't mean you can't report anything said about someone in open court. Nor does it exclude straight court reporting, provided the information used (such as names, and pieces of evidence) has not specifically been identified as being out of the public domain while a legal action is proceeding.

'You can make whatever comment you like once it's over,' says Sharpe – unless those concerned are exonerated and what you say is malicious, untrue or libellous.

- Only report provable information as fact. In other words, material you personally have evidence for.

- Base what you write on verifiable information or attributable comment.

- If you receive solicitors' letters, etc., don't ignore them.

- If you have made a mistake, own up to it.

- If you have a vested interest in a story, either make this clear, or, if there's a conflict of interest, don't write it.

- Keep notes and records for at least three years.

- Subjective comment and criticism should be treated with care – the divide between freedom of expression and character assassination isn't always clear.

- Be careful when using brand names as generic, descriptive words. Their owners can sometimes be very boring about this.

- *Sub judice* rules do not prevent reporting on legal proceedings, but writing anything that could influence those proceedings is not permissible.

Chapter 13

A VIEW FROM THE SUB'S BENCH
The experts' experts reveal all

Behind every good writer there's often an even
better rewriter. In the book trade, these people are
editors, in newspapers and magazines they're sub-editors.
The 'sub' part of their job title gives you a good indication
of the way these people earn a living. It means they're
working under editors who ultimately decide which things
make the page, and which don't.

Unedited stories are known as 'raw' copy, and some of it can be very raw indeed. The press has always been an odd melting pot of writers, from those who have an ease and facility with words to those who can barely string a sentence together, but provide something useful in terms of specialist knowledge, commentary or public profile. They might be experts on anything from chess to flower arranging, silicone breast implants to nuclear fission. The words they produce are sometimes literary mush, but it's what they say, rather than the way they say it, which is important.

Generally, a decent sub can bring a balm of reason to the most fevered paragraph, and provide a surgeon's precision to separating sentences where facts are forced together like Siamese twins.

Of course, sub-editors might not always be able to extract great literature from the enormous piles of words that are thrown at them every day, but their ability to make awful writing into something readable is often a great service to humanity.

Nor is it just obscure specialist writers who require their attentions. It's rumoured that before the lowly sub-editors have got to work on their outpourings, even some of the better known national newspaper columnists and 'name' writers' work is, shall we say, rough – although the good people are often amazingly prolific and talented.

However, in reflective, or possibly drunken, moments, sub-editors have been heard to remark that the more demanding and prima donna-ish the columnist, the worse their words.

One moderately famous hack with a regular newspaper column harangued the hapless sub who had spent many unhappy hours extracting some coherent thought from his efforts, because the man's picture byline (a postage stamp photo that went beside his name) made his shoulders 'look small'. Tempting though it would be to say that the writing underneath the picture made its author's brain look small, this was not an option. It was that sub's job to see that the words didn't. This is perhaps the literary equivalent of the person who used to follow the rag-and-bone man's horse with a shovel.

Working on the naked words of the great, the good and the not-so-good, means that sub-editors have a particular handle on the things that make good writing – which, generally speaking, means the elements they don't have to change.

To get a feeling for the mindset of this distinct journalistic breed, I persuaded two of them to talk about their careers and opinions.

In the early 1970s, David Lane was working for a regional newspaper in the English Home Counties as a junior reporter. He'd become involved in every area of the paper, and was assigned to the sub-editors' desk as part of his training. To start with he did not view the prospect with enthusiasm.

'The chief sub had a degree in Latin. He was extraordinarily pedantic for a local paper. He would have been more at home on *The Daily Telegraph*, and insisted that everything had to be absolutely kosher. One day, I put through a story which included something about erecting a building. He came round to me and said, "David, we don't have erections on the sub's table."' Of such unintended *double entendres* are working experiences made.

Mike Jones started his career as a reporter on an evening paper in Lancashire, and was attracted to sub-editing because the people he saw doing it seemed to be having a nice time. 'I used to sit on the end of the reporters' desk and watch the subs. They spent all day laughing. There were so many jokes, songs, catch-phrases and humour. They were having a ball. I went on a training course and found that I loved the work,' said Jones, who has been sub-editing UK national newspaper copy since the early 1980s.

Lane thinks the often maniacally busy period he spent as a trainee reporter, searching out stories, following them up and getting them written to deadlines, quickly and accurately, gave him a feel for good journalistic writing. So did some of the characters who trained him, including one 'hard-arsed' local newspaper editor. 'You look back on these people you might have hated at the time, and start to see what it was all about. This man was a stickler for accuracy and worked you hard. If you went to an inquest, he'd expect three stories.' This gave Lane the confidence to use his own initiative.

'For a time I worked with a manic depressive in a sprawling English new town filled with white collar industries, whose facelessness might well induce depression. He lived in a housing estate and we worked from an office in his house. One day he went to bed and just stayed there.' Without this unhappy man to mentor him, Lane had to be doubly careful that the words he filed were right.

Later he worked with a 'stringer'. The term relates to a journalist, usually self-employed, who supplies an endless stream of stories, mostly about local events that office-bound newspaper staff writers might not pick up on. 'This guy was the prince of hacks,' said Lane. 'He couldn't write, but he was a fantastic operator. The man could fish a story out of anywhere.' This ability to see something worthwhile and interesting in an event that others ignore or miss lies at the heart of a lot of successful journalistic writing, he believes.

Spending a fair amount of his early career writing, before beginning to correct other people's words, helped give Lane a well developed sense of good practice and bad. He gradually began to realise that it was his facility to work on other people's words, rather than write them himself, that represented his strongest suit. He enjoyed the discipline, and it was as a sub-editor that he began his national newspaper career. He worked for papers run by two major newspaper publishers with very different approaches, and his views on what they were looking for in their writers make interesting reading for anybody trying to break into professional writing.

'The culture of these places is very strong. Probably much bigger than the people who work for them,' he says.

Lane does not believe that writers have to bury their individual styles, saying, 'They're very much their own brand, and have styles that will stay with them all their working lives,' but reckons the ones who succeed tailor their work to suit the outlets they're writing for.

'Things are sometimes changed for subjective reasons, and any writer with an eye for longevity learns to take this in his or her stride.'

'You're looking for quality of writing expertise – for the writer to do his or her job properly. You're not a commissioning editor, you're just taking it as a piece to put in the paper, and your presence shouldn't be seen in the copy.'

This does not mean that some sub-editors' peccadilloes and personal preferences don't find their way into the stories of the writers they're editing. Things are sometimes changed for subjective reasons, which are not always logical, and any writer with an eye for longevity learns to take this in his or her stride, although when a particularly carefully crafted sentence is chopped out, this can still cause him or her to smart – something Lane is happy to concede.

When he wasn't subbing, he was frequently called to write arts reviews, some of which were cruelly hacked about by his peers. 'I was writing a review of Ultravox, a very fey 1980s' New Romantic band who were playing at the Reading Festival. They weren't going down well with the crowd, and I remember somebody chucked a bottle and it sort of floated over the audience and landed on the stage. I took some care to describe this, and the sub destroyed that phrase by changing it, and here I am, more than 20 years later, still feeling sensitive about what he did – so I do understand how writers feel.'

Jones describes his working life as 'having a certain element of creating order out of chaos. It's nice to take something, which is quite good, and make it better, or something that's appalling and make *that* better, ironing out the wrinkles and making it understandable to the reader.' He name-checks some now thoroughly famous columnists, including one who has since become a near-permanent fixture on British television, as falling into this latter category. 'Sometimes you couldn't actually tell what this person was trying to say, and it was your job to get the words to say what they wanted them to.'

Lane is happy with a story that he hasn't been forced to rip to pieces and rewrite, where he's checked the facts and found that they stand up, and if there's a query, the writer has been able to answer it. 'Ninety-eight per cent of your time is spent eliminating cock-ups, trying to make the piece accurate.'

Writers who can't work out who their audience is, irritate both men. Jones also cites individuals who spatter their work with unexplained jargon, technical and infra dig phrases.

'I think people forget that simple is good,' says Jones. 'You've got to make things unambiguous and iron out any misunderstandings that could arise.' This implies that everything is checked and nothing assumed by the writer, but a sub-editor won't automatically believe that this is the case. They constantly question, and in doing so, have helped keep generations of journalists out of the libel courts, and saved them a great deal of embarrassment or worse.

'I know of one famous film critic who got the name of a film wrong. He wasn't even close,' says Jones. Then there was the case of a television reviewer who wrote a piece round an elaborate joke about a Russian soap opera. 'Sadly, the programme was Polish.'

The things that make Lane's heart sink include obvious and easily corrected mistakes that are still in the copy by the time it reaches him, which the author should have spotted beforehand. Another annoyance is receiving acres of unwanted words.

Lane groans at the memory of this sort of thing. 'I remember someone who wrote a piece about Wagner. We wanted 3,000 words, so it was quite a long story. He must have filed 8,000. We had to shovel loads of this stuff, then spent reams of time chopping this, chopping that. Then there was the television producer who offered to write 1,500 words on a programme we were featuring. He turned in 4,000 and for a supposedly educated bloke they were all over the place – it was a very cavalier attitude.'

In the chapter on news writing ('The Basics, Part 1', pages 18–38), we looked at the curse of writers thinking their personal opinions were newsworthy, slipping them into stories. This is a regular feature of Lane and Jones' working lives. Both are likely to shudder inwardly when presented with a factual, as opposed to an opinion, piece where the word 'I' keeps cropping up.

Grammatical errors are meat and drink to both men. 'Tenses are very popular ones to get wrong,' says Jones. 'People will be veering wildly through time. You find a story that starts in the past tense and ends in the present one.'

Disentangling unfortunately-put-together sentences, which tend to reveal authors who have not properly read their copy before submitting it, is a regular feature of sub editing.

'I once had a story that said "A man arrived in a brown suit wearing a moustache",' Jones tells me. 'It's all to do with the order of ideas. The big secret is to read what you've written over and over again, and find out how anybody could see a mistake in what you've said.'

Even writers at the top of the career pile are not immune to error. A few are serial offenders. 'Some very distinguished people have huge gaps in their grammatical knowledge. They've been making the same mistakes all their lives,' suggests Jones. 'Many years ago I was privileged to sub James Cameron' (one of the last century's most accomplished news journalists and polemicists – a man for whom the word 'distinguished' could have been invented). 'If I found a mistake in James Cameron's copy, I wasn't going to ring him up about it, was I? People like that just didn't get to know [what was being done to their work].'

> **'Seeing how professional editors view a person's work will allow him or her to short-circuit mistakes before other people get to see them.'**

One element that will drive the average sub up the wall is the writer who does not read their work once it has appeared in print, assuming that what they wrote in the first place has not been changed. This was something both our sub-editors described as arrogant.

Seeing how professional editors view a person's work will allow him or her to short-circuit mistakes before other people get to see them. It also assists in picking up and eradicating serial cock-ups and bad habits, which most writers tend to develop over time. Inevitably, David Lane, Mike Jones and their colleagues are used to dealing with people who don't do this, but often take great pleasure in reading stories by those who do. Sub-editors are the literary world's mechanics, and if they don't have to fix something, the likelihood is that there probably wasn't much wrong with it in the first place.

- Sub-editors like journalists who've checked their work carefully before filing it.

- They don't like copy that is hugely over length.

- Sub-editors have saved some famous writers from going into print with awful mistakes.

- Many sub-editors are also skilled writers.

- Journalists who don't learn from changes made to their stories make sub-editors despair.

- Sub-editors often think in terms of page shapes and spaces to fill with words.

Chapter 14

WORK STATION
How to drag order from chaos

The romantic vision of retiring to an attractively chaotic writer's garret does not always translate to a pleasant reality if you're forced to do this every day. My work area/office used to be an old brick wash-house in the back garden of my home. This pleasantly ramshackle structure was used by farm workers to keep their smocks and stays clean, and had a brick floor, which sucked up moisture from the ground like blotting paper. Soon my notebooks and cuttings were getting damp and death-spot-like spores started to appear on them.

Covering the brickwork with a modern raised floor effected a cure, but with its one tiny window, which looked onto a metal coal bunker and a wooden fence, this was in fact a miserable place to work, being ill-lit, pokey and isolating. When we moved to a bigger house I commandeered an upstairs room with a decent view, to use as my home office.

The other element that did neither environment any good was the chaotic way I used them. Both doubled up as household storage areas, and in the case of the wash-house, I shared it with dismembered bits of furniture, old bicycles and garden tools. In the house-based office, I regularly tripped over a cumbersome foldaway camp bed, which was rarely used.

There were bookshelves, on which I haphazardly piled old magazines, cuttings and the books I regularly used for research. One wall was taken up by a settee bed, onto which I would sometimes fall, having collided with its foldaway cousin, in the process dislodging the piles of notes and papers.

My desk was a junk heap, with that cliché of office life, an in/out/pending tray, at one corner, groaning under yet more random paperwork and books. These flowed out onto the main desk area, burying pens and my phone number card index boxes, forcing me to stash my word processor's keyboard on the floor and work with it resting on my lap.

Lighting consisted of a harsh ceiling light and an ancient table lamp. The carpet was threadbare and stained, and the wallpaper an eye-wateringly nasty collection of 1980s' swirls.

Writing, particularly journalism (but anything involving research), generates a lot of paper – forget all the guff about paperless offices. Those who know the vagaries of computers make 'hard copies' of notes and important documents generated by them. It's also worth considering that, when confronted with a pile of A4 paper with typescript on it, and a word processor, thieves tend to ignore the paper.

Anyhow, this tide of self-generated print, along with letters and press releases, gradually took over the floor, so that just getting to my desk involved contortions. It was not an environment I enjoyed being in, and none of this helped the quality of what I wrote or my productivity.

In denial

For a long time, I resisted gentle overtures from my wife to reorganise the place, arguing with varying degrees of stupidity that I was too busy working to spend the time sorting it out or that the disruption this would involve was too awful to contemplate. Thankfully she persisted, and the place is now functional and no longer threadbare.

Under protest, I painted over the repulsive wallpaper, and laid a new carpet. Decent pictures were hung on the walls. Out went the extraneous beds, in came a bigger work-table, a decent desk, and a proper, comfortable office chair. The potential for tendon and back problems created by sitting in a slumped, uncomfortable position for long periods of time should not be underestimated. The creaking desk lamp was junked and I bought a couple of very cheap but entirely effective Ikea standard lamps, which lit the room properly, and saved my ageing eyes.

The room had ceased to be a glory hole with a word processor, and had become the place where I went to work, which was important psychologically. It was a sign that I was taking my job seriously, and had gone to the trouble to create a nice environment in which to spend most of my time during the week.

One area that still needed urgent attention was the way that I worked. Some people are naturally very organised and methodical. Others have minds like chaotic filing cabinets, something that's reflected in how they approach almost every aspect of their lives. I fall into the latter category, hence the permanent mess in my office, where I was constantly losing things. I wasted hours trying to find notebooks, press releases and cards with telephone numbers printed on them, often generating a lot of personal stress in the process.

Outside intervention

To resolve this problem I was fortunate enough to receive some outside help. I was still regularly working for a magazine that shared its office with a supplement on work and employment. One of its journalists had found a consultant who specialised in sorting out people's messy work environments, and needed a suitable subject. I was happy to volunteer.

The lady who fought her way into my office with a roll of bin-liners, a packet of sticky labels and a small notebook said she'd seen worse, before she began to systematically pull the room to pieces, asking as she picked up item after item whether I really needed it. We ended up with piles of essential stuff, useful items, things that I ought to get rid of but from which I couldn't quite bring myself to be parted, and junk, which mostly went into the bin-bags. Often labels were stuck to items so that we could decide whether they were wanted and, if so, where they belonged. I was also given my own notebook, in which I jotted down items that I needed to buy to help keep my work space in order. These included a pen holder and plastic boxes in which different magazines I regularly used for reference could be stored.

It took a morning to dismember my office, and when this was done the room seemed bigger and lighter. We then came to the crux of the way this woman worked, and the way I did not. I had to choose permanent places to keep everything I needed and used, generally putting the items which were the most important – stationery, certain reference books, etc. – within easy reach. Once they'd been used, I was to put them back, that way I'd become familiar with their locations, and would spend less time rummaging about trying to find them.

Named and retained

Since I have a sieve-like memory, every cupboard, drawer or storage box that would hide stuff was labelled with its contents, so that a rapid scan of these hiding places would tell me where something was. Before, if my memory blew a fuse, I'd have to open these things up and paw through their contents until I found the thing I needed.

Chaos theory

You might think this is obvious stuff, but it doesn't come naturally to a lot of people, and developing a system that follows that hoary old maxim, 'a place for everything, and everything in its place', is a good way of helping them to create a degree of order. A lot of people who have no aptitude for organisation really don't know where to start in creating systems that will help them, so continue as they are.

Previous attempts at ordering my work space had foundered because I did not start by purging it of superfluous things, did not work out what I needed, and did not subdivide these essentials in a simple way (i.e. books for specialist research, generic books (dictionary, etc.), reference magazines, notepads, and so on).

With outside tutoring I created subdivisions (for things like current and pending work), and cleared the mad clutter from my in/out/pending trays, promising that I would go through them on a daily basis so that their contents didn't mount up too much.

Ultimately, the way that my office has been reorganised means that I don't have to try to remember where I've put things, because they should always be in the same places. With practice, I've become familiar with those places.

Dear diary

I also have a large desk diary. This was something first forced on me by my boss at the *Evening Standard*, who'd become exasperated at my lacking a single place to forward-plan, leave messages, etc. By insisting I used a diary to do this, he did me a huge favour.

The diary allows me to jot down dates for meetings, interviews and so on, and daily chores. I spend about 10 minutes every morning making notes before I start work, and always try to have it close by, so that if I need to add a date or an aide-mémoire this can be done immediately. The book seems to plug a gap in my memory, and has reduced the horrible feeling of having forgotten something important, which had often been a part of my working life. I'm just as forgetful, but fret less because my boring-looking diary hangs onto the information my brain seems to misplace.

Its bulkiness means that it rarely leaves my office, and unlike an electronic personal organiser, it will never lose the information I've written in it. It is also harder to mislay, and is not something anybody would want to nick. OK, if my house burns down or is hit by a tidal wave I'll be in trouble, but my dull old desk diary is pretty twit-proof, and something I would now find it hard to function without.

I still generate a lot of notes and paperwork, which I sort out chronologically, putting material for each job completed into individual files before storing it in an attic, where it will be relatively easy to access if required. I throw away non-essential notes after three years.

Is my office now a paragon of neatness and organisation? Of course not – it still regresses into a paper-strewn mess – and things are still lost, but generally, they don't become *as* lost, and 10 minutes spent with a bin-bag restores order, allowing me to concentrate on writing and researching, rather than ranting and searching.

- **If you are writing at home, create a dedicated working area.**

- **Make it a pleasant environment, since you'll be spending extended periods of time there.**

- **Organise it so that every item in it has a place to live – they'll be easier to find.**

- **Deal with paperwork quickly, and try to avoid hoarding extraneous material.**

- **Keeping a desk diary allows you to plan and structure your day.**

Chapter 15

THE KEY

Forget your fears and enjoy your words

If this book has one theme, it's this: you don't
have to be a fabulous wordsmith to write well.
The best way of finding your potential as
a writer is to approach the way you work
as a professional would, which is why I've
concentrated on how journalists do things.
If you can learn to work in the
same way, whatever you write, it will
almost certainly be easier, and there's
real potential for you to improve.

I've concentrated on freelance journalists because they have to be
totally self-reliant, and because they aren't cushioned from the pitfalls
of the writing life, they are very familiar with them.

Some of the less obvious things I've covered, especially the stuff
about organising your work space and structuring the work itself, could
never be called creative, but if you're not struggling to find things from
printer ink cartridges to notebooks, or sweating over which bits of a
story to put where, then you can concentrate on making it interesting
to read. Basically, the less you have to think about peripherals, the more
you can dedicate yourself to the creative side of writing.

This is equally true whether you're writing something for a newsletter
about a village coffee morning or a story about the lives and loves of
Brazilian coffee growers.

Far from restricting you to formula writing, these things give you a framework on which to hang your ideas, rather than a cage to imprison them.

As a profession, journalism has a lousy reputation in some circles for sloppiness, inaccuracy, bias and spin. All these negatives are part of it, and always have been. However, every form of work has its charlatans, and amazingly enough, most people who write for a living are straight, scrupulously honest, care about what they do, and want to do it well. Approach what you write in the same way, and you can't lose.

Further Reading

Michael Legat, *The Nuts and Bolts of Writing* (Hale, 1989)

B.A Phythian, revised by Albert Rowe, *Teach Yourself Correct English* (Hodder Headline, 2003)

R.L. Trask, *The Penguin Guide to Punctuation* (Penguin, 1997)

Harry Blamires, *The Penguin Guide to Plain English* (Penguin, 2000)

R.L. Trask, *The Penguin Dictionary of English Grammar* (Penguin, 2000)

Daphne M. Gulland and David Hinds-Howell, *The Penguin Dictionary of English Idioms* Second edition (Penguin, 2002)

Rosalind Fergusson, *The New Penguin Dictionary of Abbreviations* (Penguin, 2000)

Elizabeth Knowles (Ed.), *The Oxford Dictionary of Quotations* (Oxford University Press, 2004)

William Strunk Jr and E.B. White, *The Elements of Style** Fourth edition (Longman, 1999)

The Writers' & Artists' Yearbook, (Published annually by A & C Black)

Linda Anderson, *Creative Writing* (Routledge, 2005)

Mike Sharples, *How We Write: Writing as Creative Design* (Routledge, 1998)

Nigel Fabb, *Sentence Structure* Second edition (Routledge, 2005)

R.W. Burchfield, *Fowlers' Modern English Usage* Third edition (Oxford University Press, 2004)

Eric Partridge, *Usage and Abusage: A Guide to Good English* (Penguin, 1999)

Sir Ernest Gowers, *Complete Plain Words* (Penguin, 1987)

Tom Welsh et al, *McNae's Essential Law for Journalists* Eighteenth edition (Oxford University Press, 2005)

Terry Darlington, *Narrow Dog to Carcassonne*** (Bantam Books, 2006)

* Recommended by Jon Courtenay Grimwood.
** A travelogue where the author has deliberately left out quotation marks.

Useful Websites

http://dir.yahoo.com/arts/humanities/literature/creative_writing
(Useful portal for finding relevant web sites)

www.freelancewriting.com
(Generic, US-based site)

www.lousywriter.com
(American site, which helps you avoid being one of its subjects)

www.oneofus.co.uk
(British-based generic site)

www.bbc.co.uk/dna/getwriting
(Helpful UK site for aspirant writers)

www.writersservices.com
(Generic site)

Index

A
accuracy 31–5
adjectives 98, 104
adverbs 99
alliteration 75
analysis pieces 39
apostrophes 78–82, 96
attributions 32, 131

B
Baker, Sue 43–4
Big Issue 16
book writing 121–2
boredom, avoiding 43–5
brand names 33–4, 133–4, 135
briefs 121
British Civil Code 130
businesses, singular or plural 102

C
Cameron, James 142
capital letters 88–90
Car 13, 14–15, 16
Chambers Concise Dictionary 70
Chapman, Giles 110, 118–20,
    121, 123–4
Classic & Sports Car magazine
    110, 119–20
clichés 63, 64, 70–7
colons 86–7
commas 84–6, 96

comment 27–9, 40
commissioning editors 106
    antagonising 108, 112
    contacting 105
        manner of approach 108
        timing 107
    developing relationship with 112
    moving on 126
    ownership of ideas 123
    replacements 126
commissions:
    fulfilling 113–14
    making changes to 114
companies, singular or plural 102
computers 145
confidence 106–7
conjunctions 100
consonants 103
contempt-of-court rules 134
contractions 80–1
copyright infringement 130, 133
Courtenay Grimwood, Jon 118,
    120, 121–2, 124
critical detachment 29–30,
    48–51
cuttings file 112

D
Daily Telegraph 16–17
dashes 94–5
defamation 130–3

delivery:
  of commissioned story 113
  dates 112
  on time 121–2
diary, using 148–9
Diesel Car 43–4
double negatives 100, 104
dyslexia 120

E
editing 17, 59–68
  in house 114
Editorial Training Consultants
  129
editors:
  see also commissioning
    editors
  antagonising 108, 112
  checking names and titles 105,
    107
  contacting 105
    manner of approach 108
    timing 107
  developing relationship with
    112
  sending material to 108–13
English language, *see also*
  language
ethics 49–51
European Court of Human
  Rights 133
Evening Standard 17, 148
exclamation marks 63, 83–4

F
failure, fear of 7, 11
feature writing 18, 39–58
  checking 67–8
  checklist 58, 69
  critical detachment 48–51
  extraneous words 54
  finding interest in subject
    43–8
  opening paragraph 41–2
  repetition of facts 53–4
  style 55–7
  using quotes in 42–3
filing 131–2
Flight International 111, 112
freelancers 10, 12–17
  checklist 124
  fears 117, 125
  flexible approach 118,
    122–3
  learning trade 119–20
  qualities 118
  self-help 117–24
  working life 125–8
full stops 82–3

G
Gilmour, David 55
Glancey, Jonathan 123
grammar 97–104, 141–2
Grimwood, Jon Courtenay 118,
  120, 121–2, 124
Guardian 16, 118, 122, 123

H
Hemingway, Ernest 8
home office 144–9
hooks 41, 109
  to attract readers 121
house style 57, 91, 101
  conforming to 109, 110
  studying details 114
hyphens 93–4

I
ideas:
  fashions in 122–4
  presentation 108–9
  recycling 123
  thinking through 108–9
Independent 43, 122
indirect questions 86
infinitives 99
  split 99
Internet 105, 122, 131, 133
interviewees:
  quotes from 126
  showing copy to 127, 128
interviews, conducting 127
introductory letters,
  following up 107
italics 90, 96

J
job files 131, 132
Jones, Mike 138, 140–2

journalism 7, 9–10
  reinventing yourself 122–3
  requirements 12–13
  route into 12–17
  saleable 123
  working life 125–8

L
Lane, David 137–40, 141, 142
language:
  achieving clarity in 23–4, 141
  misuse 59–61
  sentence structures 55
  simplicity in 52
law 129–35
learning 7–8
libel 131, 133
lighting 146
London Evening Standard 17, 148

M
Macbeth 59–60
magazines, suitable, identifying 105, 111–12
market, getting to know 111–12
Melly, George 72
mistakes:
  learning from 8
  owning up to 132, 135
Morrison, Murdo 111–12

N

names:
  of editors 105, 107
  hyphenated 94
  using correctly 33–4
negatives, double 100, 104
news stories 18–38
  accuracy in 31–5
  attributions 32
  checking and rechecking 31–2, 34–5
  checklist 38
  clarity of language in 23–4
  comments in 27–9
  critical detachment 29–30
  cutting material 22, 23
  finding interest in 21–2
  length 20
  mistakes in 35–6
  news points 18–23
    mnemonic for 19–20
  opening paragraph 20
  opinions expressed as facts 27–9
  questions about 35–6
  right to reply to 28
  sensationalising 22
  slanting 28–9
  sources 31–2
  speculation in 30–1
  taking notes for 36–7
  using first person in 141
  using quotes in 22, 25–6

notes:
  keeping 36–7, 131
  taking 127
  to organise story 52–3
nouns 97–8, 104
novels 121–2

O

Observer 43
'on spec' writing 110–11
opinions, presenting as facts 27–9
organisations, singular or plural 102
overview pieces 39
overwriting 114

P

pitching 105–16
  checklist 116
  dealing with editors 106, 107–8
  fulfilling commission 113–14
  identifying editor 105
  sending material 108–13
plagiarism 55
planning 121
possessive words 78, 79–80, 82
practice 7–9, 11
presentation 108–9
press cuttings 126
privacy 133
product journalism 48–51
pronouns 98, 104
  possessive 79–80, 98

public interest 130–1
public relations people 48–50
punctuation 23–4, 78–96
  checklist 96

Q
question marks 83, 96
questions, indirect 86
quotation marks 91–2, 96
quotes 22, 25–6, 42–3
  keeping records of 36–7, 131–2
  punctuation before 92
  reproducing 126

R
reading aloud 15, 67
rejection, reducing stress of 107
Rendell, Ruth 7
repetition:
  of facts 53–4
  of words 63, 66–7
research 22
rewrites 15
Reynolds, Albert 130
Reynolds Defence 130–1
rhythm, in writing 55, 65–6
Rook, Jean 109

S
SAGA Magazine 43–4
semicolons 87
sentences:
  cherished 68

clumsy 61–5
  mixed up 141
  pace 65–6
  rhythm 55, 65–6
  structure, repeating 55
Shakespeare, William 59–60
Sharpe, Richard 33, 129–30,
  132, 133, 134
slander 130
solicitor's letter, receiving 132
specialist terms, explaining 51–2
speculation 30–1
speech marks see quotation
  marks
spelling 102–3, 104
  of names 33–4
split infinitives 99
standards, maintaining 43–5, 126
standfirsts 119
stress, reducing 107
stringer 138
sub judice 130, 134
sub-editors 136–43
Sunday Times 130–1
Swengley, Nicole 125–7

T
tabloids 20–1
tenses 100–1
titles, personal, use of 32–3
trade magazines 16
trademarked names 33–4, 133–4,
  135

U
unsolicited material 109–10

V
verbs 99, 104
  singular and plural 101–2
  tenses 100–1
vowels 103–4

W
websites 154
Wolmar, Christian 43
Woolf Reforms 130
words:
  capitalisation 89–90
  contractions 80–1
  extraneous, purging 54

harkneyed 71–6
misuse 59–61
repetition 52, 66–7
work place 144–9
  organising 146–8
working life 125–8
writer:
  becoming 12–17
  getting established as 114–15
Writers' and Artists' Yearbook
  105
writing:
  critics of 6–7
  fashions in 122–3
  planning 121
  style 55–7
  truth about 6–11

Acknowledgements

Thanks to editors Gareth Jones and Kate Parker, copy editor Simon Pooley, and New Holland authority figure Rosemary Wilkinson. Nigel Wigmore, Giles Chapman, Nicole Swengley, Jon Courtenay Grimwood, Andrew Barry-Purssell, Mic Cheetham, David, Jenny and as ever, Jane, my word-count-weary wife.